IT'S OUR BLEND THAT MAKES US OUTSTANDING

POETRY AND PROSE

By

Thomas L. Poteet

ALSO BY TOM POTEET

SING A NEW PSALM

THE WINDS OF CHANGE – MAKING IT THROUGH

HOLD THEM EACH IN YOUR LOVING ARMS

FOR A SEASON – THE OTHER POEMS

DEDICATED TO HOPE:
That never-ending Source of Nourishment

TABLE OF CONTENTS

INTRODUCTION

I have been trying to convince anyone, who will listen, for decades, that we are all equal; that no matter our nationality, race, sex or religion, we are all children of the Most-High God; whether we believe in God or not.

I feel like I have been working to convince others of this truth for more than thirty years. You may think that the pages, before you, are not much to show for a thirty-year effort; but the need to expound and to convince others that we are all equal, that our blend of nationality, race, sex and religion brings beauty to our humanity, has been on my mind (if not on paper) for a long time.

I have included, in this book, poems written since the early 1990's. These poems span decades of thought and words placed on a page. I believe my thoughts and expressions have stayed true over the years. I may have changed my mind, during this time, on some things; but my thoughts on equality have stayed the same. They are continuous and consistent.

I also have included some commentary on my poems. Poems mean different things to different people, in different places and over different times. I understand that. It is what makes poetry so special. I thought it prudent, however, with the poems included, to explain some of my thoughts; thoughts as I wrote; and thoughts as I peruse again.

I have spent the last few decades of my life writing, mostly in the early morning. I would begin the morning writing process in prayer to my Lord for getting me through the previous day; then continue my prayers for preparing me for the day to come. It was my time of peace. I found that my morning prayers flowed in a more coherent pattern as I prayed; and my prayers eventually became my poems. I could see how His Words became mine through my filters. I could better face each day knowing He Was With me. There is no better way for me to begin each day.

Throughout these decades, my prayers and thoughts, combined with His Leading, have led me to this place and time; where I understand better the meaning of who I am and Whose I am. My parents were good and honest people. They loved me and my two brothers. They loved their grandchildren and great-grandchildren. They taught me what love is; but not the width and depth and breadth of what Love is. Though I never heard a word of bigotry escape my dad's mouth, that was not the case for all of the members of our family and extended family. It wasn't until I fully realized that I was a child of the Most-High God, as were all of His children, that I knew that we have one Parent, the Father of us all; whether we recognize Him or speak with Him or even have ever come to know Him. We have one Father and we are all His children. We are to love Him with all of our heart, mind, soul and strength; and we are to love our neighbors (His children) as we love ourself; even as He Loves us.

Throughout my years of prayers and writing, I have become more and more aware of all of the inequalities we seem to see; and the equality we should be seeing. My hope is that I can, with the following poems and prose, present a better picture of what I'm seeing.

CHAPTER 1 - OUR BLEND

OH, PATCH OF WILDFLOWERS

Oh, patch
Of wildflowers,
Growing as if
You were unattended.

Your colors
Are wonderful;
Your shades
Are precious;
Your blend
Is beautiful;
You are short
And tall
And of many hues;
You bend differently
As the breeze
Passes you by.

The weeds
Are intermingled
Here and there
But you
Do not seem
To care.

You are so
Much more
Together
Than apart;
And though
You are each
Precious
In our sight,
It is your blend
That makes you
Outstanding.

I begin with a poem I wrote in the early 1990's. I have written other poems about the beauty of flowers; but I still like this one best.

I planted a patch of wildflowers behind our garden way back when. I started them from seeds. I really didn't think they would do much the first year; but they did. They were spectacular; eventually spreading over the last row of plants in our garden. The blend of size and type and color were remarkable to me. I watched their growth each day. I enjoyed their beauty each day. They gave me both joy and peace. They inspired me to write the poem above; though my thoughts were as much on humanity as they were on the wildflowers. A beautiful metaphor should not be wasted.

PEACE WE'LL FIND

Some flowers
Bloom
At night.

Some flowers
Bloom
In light.

Whenever
They decide
To bloom,
They bring me
Such delight.

The colors
Blend
For all.

I do not
Force
Their call.

All hues arrive
Under
My sky;

My motion
Seems to stall.

I stare
At beauty
Here.

I stare
At color
Dear.

I can't
Let go;
The colors flow
Across the palette
Near.

Why can't
We be
As they?

Let colors
Lead
The way?

Our beauty
Blends;
His Colors send;
And peace we'll find
Today.

Another poem about the beauty of blending; and the peace that the blending of color can give. I stated, in the beginning poem, that weeds do not get in the way of flowers. Weeds can steal moisture from flowers; but they seldom diminish the flowers' beauty. Weeds are a powerful metaphor, to me at least, of all of the things that detract from our beauty together. Whether those distractions are worries and concerns, thoughts or greed. There are so many distractions; including not wanting to see past the distractions. Beauty exists, however, among and through our distractions. We can see the beauty if we wish to see the beauty. With beauty comes peace; whether that beauty comes from flowers, art, music, writing, family, friends, or just that special someone. We can find beauty. It is there.

THEY WERE ALL IMPORTANT

As I watched the symphony,
I noticed the preponderance
Of violins and violas;
So many more were they
Than the others.

There were rows and rows,
But only a few bassoons
And not many oboes;
A few flutes,
Trumpets and trombones;
Some cellos;
Only one piano, a harp
And some percussion.

I should not
Have heard the others.

They should have been
Blotted out
By the violins and violas;
But they weren't.

As the conductor began,
He pointed to this group
And that;
He waved his arms
Over all
As he blended
Each and every instrument
Into one wonderful voice.

If I listened carefully,
I could hear each instrument,

Though I preferred
To listen to them all
With such clarity
And brilliance.

When it was over,
He took a bow;
Then asked each to stand
As one body;
For they were all important.

I turn now to the blend of a symphony orchestra.

In my much earlier years, I played the saxophone. I played in the
Junior High (now Middle) school concert band; then I played in the
High School concert band. Instead of violins, there were clarinets; but
the rules of engagement were the same as a symphony orchestra.
Through the years, our son played the trumpet in the high school
concert band; our grandchildren have played the flute, the trumpet, the
saxophone and percussion in their respective school bands. We have
been to many school concerts and professional symphonies. I have
always loved the experience.

I must admit that the maturity of the players becomes evident as they
move from elementary school to middle school to high school to
college; and then to the professional stage. Learning to play and read
music is one thing. Learning to follow the conductor is quite another.
As the members of the band or orchestra mature, they learn the music
better and they can more and more concentrate on the conductor. The
focus shifts from friends and family, in the audience, to the conductor
standing before them. The music, coming from the instruments, is
beautiful; but it is the conductor that blends them all together in a way
that transcends each individual instrument; and the notes that each
instrument play.

CONSIDER THE LILIES

Consider the lilies,
How they bloom;
Bringing beauty

Next to gloom.

How their colors
Stand alone,
Whether crowded
Or as one.

They blend with others
And themselves;
They add their beauty
To all else.

They grow in stones;
They grow in clay;
They grow in water;
They bloom all day.

I cannot wait,
With the rising moon,
For the morning
To see new blooms.

I think that we
Should be as they;
Bringing beauty
To each day.

Consider the lilies,
How they bloom;
See their beauty
Erase the gloom.

THE LILIES AND WEEDS

The lilies and weeds
Get along;
The roots of the lilies
Are that strong.

No need to free

The lilies from the weeds;
Their beauty will shine
With little met needs.

One of my favorite perennials is the daylily. Since I first planted them
in our garden in the early 1970's, I have loved them. My brother first
gave me some orange and brown daylilies, which I planted in our
garden. Then a woman at church, whose name was actually Mrs.
Flowers, gave us some yellow daylilies, which I planted next to those
from my brother. They grew so well that I had to separate them and
plant them in other locations; including within the evergreens at the
back of the property; and around the pond. During their summer
bloom, I would marvel at their beauty; how they would bloom in poor
soil; even under water. They reminded me, so often, of how we can
share our beauty no matter where we are. Again, it is their blend and
strength, together, that make them so beautiful and so resilient.

CHAPTER 2 - OUR STRUGGLE

YOUR DELICATE PERSISTENCE

Delicate petunia,
Discarded in the pile
Of dead weeds;
Plucked because
You were ungainly,
Not pretty
Anymore.

How you struggle
In the box
Of weeds,
Gathering strength
From who knows where.

Your roots
Have been severed;
Yet you still bloom,
Though faintly.

Discarded,
Not loved,
Left to fend
For yourself,
Your color is pale;
Yet you still fight
To stay alive.

I,
Who have so much,
Long for
Your delicate persistence.

There is beauty in our blend; but there is struggle in our loneliness; when we do not feel we belong to those beautiful wildflowers or that talented orchestra.

So many of my poems were written in the early 1990's. This, too, is one of them.

We had pulled up some withered annuals from our gardens, along with the encroaching weeds, toward the end of the summer growing season. It was fall clean-up time. I was more interested in cleaning up and making the outside look more presentable. I preferred not looking at the weeds which were taking over the flower beds. I had all of the weeds packed in a large cardboard box; and the box was sitting by the trash cans at the back of the house. When I got ready to take that box of weeds back to the back of the property, I noticed a petunia with a faint blue bloom. Another metaphor stared me in the face. I noted then, as I remember now, that we tend to discard the poor, the homeless, the disenfranchised. We don't wish to see the many who struggle as part of our Father's family, as a brother or sister of worth. We tend to think they have nothing to offer; but, of course, they do. They can add to our lives if we let them.

SOMEWHERE IN THE COSMOS

Somewhere in the cosmos
A lily is blooming.

I cannot see it.

The wildflowers
Are hiding
Its existence.

I see its stem
But not its bloom.

Yet
I sense its bloom
As clearly
As I see the others
Which are framed
By the foliage.

The ones I see

Delight my eye;
The one I can't see
Makes me sigh.

The ones I see
Like painted blooms;
The one I can't see
Sings these tunes.

I am dazzled
By their beauty;
I am impressed
With blooms profuse;
I am delighted
They appeared at all
Midst this summer
Of abuse.

But the lily
I cannot see
Delights me most;
For it blooms
Without a care
Of who is there.

It blooms
Though no one
Can ever see
The delight
It is to be.

Somewhere in the Cosmos
A lily is blooming . . .

My Mom gave me some lilies, from her backyard, at a time when we lived in the country with our three sons; and had a fairly large vegetable garden. As the boys grew, our income increased, and the need for volumes of vegetables decreased, I used some of the space, previously used for vegetables, for some flowers. Those flowers included the daylilies mentioned above. I wanted the flowers to add some color as the summer wore on. I planted Mom's lilies toward the back of the garden, right in front of and before I planted the wildflowers previously mentioned. Mom called her lilies crazy lilies. Each stalk had a single bloom, a bloom that lasted weeks; unlike the other daylilies in the garden, whose many blooms lasted only a day. These lilies bloomed for a couple of years before I decided to plant the row of wildflowers immediately behind the garden.

I had no idea how fast and how large the cosmos would grow among the other wildflowers. They were beautiful; but they grew so large that they began to cover over some of the crazy lilies as they were still blooming. I stood, one sunny day, looking over the beauty of the flowers, and noticed that the cosmos was taking over. I got down on one knee and saw a single crazy lily still blooming under the canopy of the cosmos. That is when the poem above came to be. I've thought of this poem often when a hidden talent has come forth, whether on a TV show or on social media. I have thought, so often, what we miss when we disparage an individual due to race or nationality or religion. For there are so many gifts we miss when we do not recognize the talents or gifts of another simply because we do not value their place of birth or their beliefs; simply because we do not get down on our knees to truly see them.

WHEN ONE OF THE MEMBERS

Something
Bit my forearm
Causing it to swell
And become inflamed.

I could not determine
The cause;
Only the reaction.

The rest of me
Became weak
With fever.

Though
I needed sleep

I could not rest.

Then the Doc
Gave me an antibiotic
Which killed
The toxin
And brought order
To the system.

When one of the members
Is infected
It takes the others
With them.

I conclude this chapter with the danger caused when an individual, or group of individuals, decide to disparage the beauty of the blend of humanity. I use the metaphor of a spider bite, which sent me to the doctor's office so many years ago.

We need to be careful to whom we listen. There is so much hate lurking about, ready to infect a world that can be quite beautiful if we see it for its beauty, not its ugliness. Our blending is so important to our success, to our beauty and to our resilience. But there are some who would prefer to divide us, to concentrate on one flower over the rest, on one instrument over the rest. They want to conduct our life to their own music of discord. When we allow divisiveness (weeds) to take over our thoughts, the infection grows.

CHAPTER 3 - EQUALITY

I AM A CHILD

I am a child
Of the Most High God.

My color,
My age,
My sex,
My education,
My job,
My creed
Are not the requirements
I need
To move on.

Only
That I am
His child.

But I cannot
Be His child
If I treat not
My siblings
As my equals;
For they
Are His children too.

Their color,
Their age,
Their sex,
Their education,
Their job,
Their creed
Are not the requirements
I need
To love them.

Only
That they
Are His children.

To love Him
And His children
Are our greatest
Commandments.

Adding His Grace
Puts it all
Into place.

I hope that my transition, here, from flowers, orchestras and spider bites to the human condition, will make some sense. For, again, my point is that our human existence requires a blend of nationalities, religions, sexes and races to be its best. Humanity requires each of us to accept everyone of us; for without our differences, we will never learn. If we do not learn, we will never grow.

My story is unique to me; as everyone's story is unique to them. For example, I did not choose when and where I was born. I did not choose to be born in 1946 in a suburb right outside the Baltimore City boundaries. I did not choose to be born to blue-collar parents in a mostly blue-collar neighborhood. I did not choose the type of house nor the small yard where I would be raised. I did not choose the Lutheran Church, where I would later attend Sunday School. I did not choose to go to the elementary school a block away, or the junior high school or high school that were all within walking distance. I did not choose my DNA; nor did my ancestors. I did not choose any of these things.

I was born in the time and at the place I was born. It's that simple. I was born to the parents who chose to have another child after their doctor said it would be a good idea because of the death of their first child to polio. He is the older brother I never had the pleasure to meet; though his picture holds an esteemed place in my office. Every time I look at his picture, I am reminded that I am here because he is not.

I was born to replace another; and to add to two older brothers; and to make a family of five. I did not choose this option. I came into a loving family, which was fortunate for me; because that is not always the case.

I say all of this because no one chooses their time or place to be born. No one chooses the mores at the time when or place where they will get their start. No one chooses their parents beliefs. No one chooses the color of their skin. No one chooses to come into a family full of or devoid of love.

Yet we tend to look at the color of an individual's skin or the place in the world that they call home or the religious beliefs by which they were raised; and we determine whether we are better than they are; or maybe that we are not as good as they are; even though we are all children of the Most-High God; and we are all Loved the same.

HOW DARE WE COMPARE?

How dare
We compare
Our lives
With theirs.

Do we have
Any semblance
Of their upbringing?

Do we have
Any idea
What thoughts
Crossed their minds;
Or if ever
There was a tear
As they moved
From year to year?

Do we know
What they perceived
As real?

Have we felt
The pain
They for certain did feel?

How can
We make decisions
For lives
That are not ours?

Are we willing
To pay
The consequences?

Who are we
To play God
With the decisions
They make
From derision?

We are not
Their Creator
Nor Redeemer.

Who are we
To know
What they feel?

Who are we
To know what to them
Is so real?

WHO ARE WE?

Who are we
To see through you?

Have we nothing better
To do?

Why do we take time

To judge
While from our faults
We do not budge?

When will we take time
To cure
Our pompous thoughts
Which make us bore?

Where were we
While you spent your life
Struggling through
Each year of strife?

How do we know
Your destiny
With our two eyes
Too blind to see?

I question why we want to question. We all want to be a judge. We want to criticize someone else concerning the color of their skin, their hair style, their manner of dress, the way they act, where they go to worship, what they do when they don't go to worship. So many countless ways we wish to judge another's life and lifestyle.

I'm not sure why we think we are so righteous that we can sit, in judgement, of someone else. We did not grow up in their particular family. We do not know what trials and tribulations they have encountered. I guess we want for everyone to be like us. They would probably like the same. But it doesn't work that way. We are all different; even our siblings in our own family. We're not always crazy about the members of our own family; but we normally do not wish harm to come to them. We love them even if we don't always like them. Why can't we extend that principle to all of the children of our Father?

WE ARE ALL ONE

We are all one;
Each of us connected.

We are all siblings;
Whether
We love
Or hate
Our sisters and brothers
Does not change
The Truth.

We have One Parent;
One Who Grieves
When we treat each other
With disdain;
One Who Grieves
When a child
Has no chance
Due to hatred
And violence.

We are all one;
Each of us connected.

When one dies
Because
Of our lies,
The whole
Is lessened;
So hard to build
When we are set
On destruction.

To respect
Our siblings,
Not to neglect
Their plea,
Is how the Universe
Expects
To be.

WE ARE TO LIVE

What divides
Does not unite.

What takes away
Does not add.

We are to live
As a family;
But we do not.

We are to love
Our siblings;
But we don't.

How is it
We have One Father,
Yet we see Him
So differently?

If He is One
Then should He not
Be the Same
For all?

We act
As if we're special.

We believe
He loves us best.

So we take
What we believe
And we put it
To the test.

We divide
His very family.

We subtract
From all the rest.

We withhold
The Love
He gives us.

We have made
This world
A mess.

My thoughts always go to loving our neighbors as we love ourselves. I can understand, a little, how we can hate our neighbor if we hate ourself. That makes some sense; and probably explains some of what is happening in this world. My parents taught us to love; to love who we are; to love those around us; to respect those around us. But some parents don't teach those basics.

The greatest commandment, to love the Lord God with all of our heart, mind, soul and strength, is followed by another great commandment, to love our neighbors as ourselves. The first part is fairly easy for anyone of faith. The second is so much harder. When my Lord was asked the question of who is our neighbor, the answer probably did not sit well with the audience. The audience expected the definition of neighbor to be someone like them. My Lord's definition of neighbor, however, was someone different from the audience. My Lord's definition was someone from a different place and with different religious beliefs. Many still do not like His answer.

WITHOUT ONE FATHER

My brothers and I talk;
But not often.

There is a feeling
Of comfort
We have
In each other.

Though times
Have come,

And will again,
When we rallied
For each other,
Years pass;
Yet we sense
An attachment.

Mom and dad,
Along with
A common household,
Are our glue.

We are united
With them
And through them.

Some memories
We share;
Though from different
Perspectives.

Through time
We have honored
Each other.

We have been
Unselfish
In our fashion.

We have laughed
Together
And cried
Together.

We have weathered storms
And played
Under starry skies.

I would be less
Of who I am

Without them.

If we had come
From different families
It would not
Be the same.

Without one Father
There is no meaning
To the brotherhood
Of man.

FAMILY

Family
Can be
So hard.

The closer
We are
Can push us far
Away.

We are not alike
Though our genes
May be;
We may look similar
Within
Our family tree.

But there are
Differences
In how we view;
Differences
In our attitude;
Differences
In our beliefs;
Differences
In our bequeaths.

We do not know
How love can grow
Through the differences
That we bestow.

But try we must,
Though hard to be,
To keep all limbs
On the family tree;
And try we must,
If peace to find,
When members fly
With thoughts so blind.

How can there be
Any peace on earth
If families neglect
To find it first?

The first poem, above, was written before my oldest brother's death. There are only two of us brothers remaining. We still don't speak to each other very often. We do send cards at birthdays and Christmas. We still acknowledge each other as brothers; but we do not live close, our interests are different; we have no friends in common; our parents are no longer here for family gatherings. We have gone our separate ways; like old lions. We have always loved each other; but we have not always liked what each other was doing. That said, we have never wished any harm to each other. We have never wished bad to befall each other. When something went wrong with the other, we were always there to support. As long as we are both alive, we will always support each other.

Family is hard. The older we grow, the farther away we move makes it more difficult to stay in touch; even with the communication devices we now have. There are certainly some families who stay close together; and that is wonderful. Many, however, do not stay close; and friction (weeds) tends to grow among them. It is hard, so often, to remain in love with our family. It is worth it simply for the moments of beauty that come to light.

A GIFT OF LOVE

A gift of love
Is what we are;
A gift to each other;
Each sister and brother.

Each gift is wrapped
In different ways;
In different styles;
In different shades;
But all are beautiful
In His View.

Our gift of love
We need to share;
Our gift of love
We need to bear
For all to see
So all can be
In His Grace.

A gift of love
Is what we are;
A gift to share
And travel far
To those in need
As they succeed
To share
Their gifts as well.

We need not wait,
Not hesitate
To share our gift,
Each precious gift,
To all who need,
To all who feed
On Love Divine;
That love

Of yours and mine
To share.

At the funeral of a favorite uncle, the minister reflected that this gentleman was a gift of love to the world. I believe we all are.

NOT A CONTEST

Life
Is not
A contest.

Not
Between you
And me.

That is not
How
It is to be.

I
Do not win
If
You lose.

A winner
I am not
To choose.

We
Are sisters
And brothers.

We
Do not gloat
At misfortunes
Of others.

There is no pride
If

You lose it
All.

There is no pride
If
I let you
Fall.

It is we
Through
This journey
He Sees.

It is we
Who
Cross the line
Together;
We
Who
Our paths
Are tethered.

We
Run together
If
We choose.

If not,
We
Will choose
To lose.

WE ALL POINT

We all point
At each other
As if there's one
To blame;
But
We are all

In this world
Together;
And He Loves each one
The same.

We are all different; yet we are all equal. Because we are different, I
guess, we want others to see that we are the best. So we compete; no
matter where we compete; at home, at play, on the job. We tend to
think we have to win in order to get ahead. If that means putting
another down or demeaning them. We want to feel we are superior. It
is easier then to step over them to continue our path to glory. We want
to cast blame. We want to say we've done nothing wrong; that it's all
the other person's fault. We have it all wrong. We are all servants on
this earth. We are not masters.

THE GOLDEN RULE

We learn
The golden rule
By living
The golden rule;
Not by reciting
The golden rule.

Not tradition,
Nor ceremony,
Nor creed
Can replace
The lack
Of true compassion
And love
For our sisters
And brothers.

I have heard "The Golden Rule" mentioned since I was very young. It
is a beautiful rule; full of fairness and goodness. It is a blessed rule.
But it is a rule that applies to both the speaker and to those to whom
the speaker is addressing. It applies to all.

THE SAME FAMILY

We are different;
Yet equal.

Our paths
Are not the same;
Yet
They should lead
To one destination:
A Mansion Room
Where we can bloom
Together.

I am
Our Father's child;
As are you.

We are of
The same Family.

So much more
We need to do
Together.

My premise, for equality, begins with the understanding that we all
have one Father. I guess there are other ways to get to the fact that we
are all brothers and sisters. I simply can't get to that Truth without His
Truth.

HIS LOVE

We cannot make
Another
Love us;
But,
We can love
Them.

There is no

Weapon
At our head
To force us
To hate.

There is no
Path
At our feet
Which forces
Our way
To defeat.

No other
Had more reason
For vengeance
Than my Lord.

No other,
More worthy,
Had more despise
Cast
In their eyes
Than He
Who leads me.

Only Love
Can cast out
Hate.

Only Love
Can cast out
Evil.

I feel
His Life Blood
Flow.

His Love
Is all I need
To know.

I have spent so much of my last thirty-years in prayer. My writing comes from those prayers; and the feelings and sensations I receive while praying. I have attempted to explain, in the past, that we only come to know another through being with them; and conversing with them; and sharing with them. That is what prayer has become for me: conversation with my Lord. The fact that He already Knows what is on my mind does not deter me from sharing my thoughts with Him; and my love for Him. I feel His Life Blood flow/His Love is all I need to know.

CHAPTER 4 - PRAYERS FOR OTHERS

Throughout my years of writing, I have begun with prayer. I would start, each morning, by simply praying; and quickly realize I had better write down what was going through my mind. The following are some of those prayers that reinforced my thoughts about brothers and sisters and neighbors. They are prayers from us for them. I thought maybe that the following prayers might help you to begin a prayer all your own.

NEIGHBORS

Thank You, Father,
For neighbors
Who sense a need.

Thank You, Father,
For neighbors
Who have no greed;
Who ask for nothing
For the favors
They bestow;
Who do their good,
Then move along;
Leaving You to know
The burdens lifted
As they go.

Thank You, Father,
For sending them
Along.

Thank You, Father,
For choosing
From the throng
A few
Who do not care
For treasures;
A few
Who look not

To the measures
Of their reward;
Yet for someone else
They look toward.

Thank You, Father,
For neighbors
So quiet, yet true.

Thank You, Father,
For the strong, yet few,
Who do for others
And so do for You.

PROTECT MY SIBLINGS

Please, Lord,
Protect my siblings
In Ways
Unknown.

Please
Let them see
How in You
We've grown.

Hold them each
In Your Loving Arms.

Protect them please
From all earthly harms.

Please, Lord,
Walk with them
Though
They may not know.

Watch their path
Wherever
They may go.

Bring them home
When they lose their way.

Show Your Light
Throughout their day.

Please, Lord,
Place Your Hand
On
Their fevered head.

Sit with them
When
They're full of dread.

Hold their hand
When
They won't get up.

Cry with them
When
They drink of Your Cup.

Please, Lord,
Bless my siblings;
This I pray:
Show Your Light
While they walk
In gray.

A PRAYER

Father,
Reach down
Through his fear
And pain
And help him see
Your Face
Again;

For throughout
The struggle
You remain
The only strength
He can regain.

HOPE

Thank You
For hope;
That never-ending
Source
Of nourishment
That allows us
Entry
Into dreams
Of
Another time
And place;
When all
Is at peace
In
Our minds
And in
Our souls.

IN VIEW

Ever increase
Those things
In us
That we see
In You;
For when
We dare
To try
To hold You
In view,
We see
Perfection

In each
Direction.

And though
We may
Not know
How to reach;
Yet we know
You will teach
Our hearts
And minds
If we
But take
The time
To keep You
In view.

CHAPTER 5 - PRAYERS FOR SELF

I have written prayers for others and prayers for myself. I share my prayers for self with you; remembering that we have to put our own oxygen mask on before we put one on another; remembering that we need to love ourselves before we can learn to love another.

LET ME REFLECT (A Prayer)

Father,
Bring Your Love
Divine
Into
This stagnant heart
Of mine.

Bring forth
Your Grace
To light
This face
As I reflect
Without neglect.

Give me courage
To let life flow
Into the hearts
I've come to know.

And when this light
Inside
Is snuffed,
Let me reflect
I've done enough.

IN EVERY WAY

Everyday
In every way
Help me to be
And to do

The best I can
For You.

Help me
To be strong.

Give me
The courage
To move along
In Your Path
Till I reach You
At last.

Help me
To be patient.

Let each minute
Of each day
Not sway
My mind
From thoughts
Sublime.

Help me
To be wise.

Grant that I
May see
And teach
With clarity
The View
You Wish to Be.

Help me
To have mercy.

Let me
Not judge
Nor rule Your child
Who wishes

To escape
From a world so wild.

Everyday
In every way
Help me to be
What You See
For me.

IT'S OK TO STAY

Father,
Give me peace,
I pray.

See me through
Each day.

Right me
When I fall.

Help me love
Them all.

Give me patience,
Lord.

Cling me to
Your Word.

Let me drift
Not much.

Help me search
Your Touch.

When I lose
My way,
Grab my hand
And Say,

It's OK
To stay
By Your Side.

SEA OF CONFUSION

Help me
To get my mind
Off of me
And onto
What You see
As the needs
Of my brothers
And sisters.

Help me
To guide
My energies
To those
Around me
So I can be
What You want me
To be;
And not flounder
In my own
Sea of confusion.

A prayer that I have prayed so often:

THE REST OF OUR BOOK

Father, let me clear my mind
Of what's behind
And forward look
To the rest of our book.

Let me focus,
As I should,
On what's ahead
So full of good.

Let me leave
All of my past
That in Your Mind
Will never last.

Give me stamina
And energy
To scale the slopes
In front of me;
And when
I reach the top
Do not allow
My guard to drop.

Let Your Children
Hear You clear
Through the words
You write so dear
With the pen
That's in my hand
That each morning
You demand.

Let my tiredness
Not disdain
The words
You would proclaim;
But let me rise
Each morn in joy
With the gifts
That You employ.

And help me see
What lies ahead
Of Your Beauty
In my head;
And let me face
Your World Unknown
With the Love

In which I've grown.

CHAPTER 6 - MY TEACHER

I did not come to the ideas and thoughts above by myself. I had a great deal of help. My Teacher is flawless. He Lived for all of us thousands of years ago. He Lives in each of us now. Many do not know Him as I do; and many will ever refuse to know Him as I do. I have conversed with Him for so many years; and I have come to know Him well.

The words I write are not wholly mine. They come from a source I cannot see; yet I feel so real. My writing is not always a spiritual thing. I simply sit and write. The words appear on the page. It is not some illusion. I am not a channel. I write what comes to me through the filters I have acquired over the years. Though I have a lot of help.

HIS WORK

I sit
With a host of angels
And write
With a hand of man.

I am surprised
At what I see
Flow forth
From inside me.

I read
And comprehend
While I write
The words He sends.

I read them all
Again and again
As my soul
Begins to mend.

Such a joy
To see it flow;
These words
I've come to know.

I am lifted
To a plane
Which resolves
All of my pain.

It is pleasant here
As they are near
To feed my soul
With Love so dear.

I have no fear
Of what comes next
As they enjoy
Our flow of text.

No glory
Do I need to see;
Only knowing
That they sit by me.

IN EVERY WAY

I sit alone,
But not alone.

He sits with me
In my home
Far away
From Home;
So,
I am not alone.

I feel His Presence
In all I do.

He speaks through me
And sees me through
Another day
In every way.

I love Him so.

I tell Him so.

I sing His praise
And am amazed
As all the blessings
Come my way.

So hard to understand,
As He takes my hand,
That I am just one man.

For His family
Are as the stars
In the sky;
Yet,
He is Here
To help me by
And place a smile
Instead of a sigh.

I sit alone,
But not alone.

He sits with me
As He sits with you
And He will see you through
Another day
In every way.

My teacher led a perfect life. I do not. I have my problems, my biases, my ill-conceived thoughts. From all I have read; from all of the conversations I have had with Him, He did not and does not have my issues. Though I will never be perfect; nor always have wonderful, beautiful thoughts, I can still strive to be like my teacher. I can do my best to be like Him.

WHY CAN'T WE?

Why can't we
Be as He;
Content to serve
Our siblings
In kindness
And understanding?

Why can't we
See as He;
To a future
In Mansions
Of Glory
In His Presence?

Why can't we
Hear as He;
And follow
The Will
Of our Father
In Heaven?

Why can't we
Be as He;
Not talking about
Our siblings,
But listening
To their concerns?

We are meant to be
As He;
Though not Perfect,
We can still try
To follow His Lead.

DOING GOOD

He went about
Doing good.

He was in no hurry.

He stopped
And helped
And loved
All those who approached;
Even those who perched
In a tree.

As He passed by
He showered blessings
To all who came
Into His Midst.

It mattered not
Male or female,
Jew or Gentile,
Color of skin.

It mattered not
That they may be despised
By His own earthly religion;
Or that they may be sick
Or slowly eaten away
By leprosy
Or hatred.

He went about
Doing good.

As He ate
And walked
And worshipped,
No place
Was the wrong place
Or inconvenient place
To show Love
And Compassion.

A true lesson
He gave us
For all time:
To go about
Doing good
As we pass by.

WHY CAN'T WE?

Why can't we
Be more like Him?

Why can't we
Laugh at insults
And turn them
Into lessons
For the masses?

Why can't we
Be offended
With grace
And take our punches
With dignity?

Why can't we
Be kind to others
With whom
We disagree;
Or touch the unclean
Who need our touch
So very much?

How
Can we atone
For walking
All alone,
Or in a crowd
Of minds
All
Of one kind?

Why can't we
Be more like Him?

He spoke to all
And touched all
And never feared
What others thought.

And He paid the price
With Forgiveness
In His Heart.

MY HERO

To follow
A lesser life
Would be
To miss the mark.

To set before me
A hero
Less than perfect
Would allow me
To excuse
My imperfections;
Would allow me
To say
There's no other way.

So I ascend
The highest peak,
Not for the weak,
Where peace
Is but a vision.

My ascent is rife
With strife
As I attempt
This fuller life
Of service.

For I must dig
To the depths
To reach
The heights.

Each motive
Must be weighed
Before my actions
Are conveyed.

And thought
Must always
Come before
The instincts
I explore.

My Hero
Is Perfect,
You see,
And less
Would never do
For me.

THE RAINBOWS OF OUR SOULS

Heartaches come
In many colors.

Though ours may blend,
They may never match
Another's.

Though we may share,
We will never know
Their sorrow.

Only our Lord knows
The rainbows
Of our souls.

HE LOOKS AFTER ME

He looks after me.

Far and away
He sees better than I see.

He comforts me.

Sitting miles
From home
He lets me know
I'm not alone.

With visions
In my head
He leads me to hope
Instead of dread.

Always mindful
He pushes me ahead.

I am renewed.

With borrowed strength
I change my attitude.

From lost to found
I gain some ground
Which leads me to
A path that's sound;
Where dreams
Overflowing abound.

He allows me
To escape
These mundane walls
And leads me to
His Hallowed Halls
Of Love;

So Great
It can only be viewed
From Above.

From Hallowed Halls
I'm able to see
The Glorious Love
In front of me;
A Place
Where I can be
Someday;
A Place
So bountiful
That I pray
To see once more
The dreams
That I adore.

The following two poems have always been hard for me. They have caused me much pain; but they are a large part of how I see my teacher. My teacher led. He did not follow His own path. He followed the path of His Father; our Father. My teacher led so that I can follow. I could have used nicer words in "The Message of the Cross". I could have used "persecute" instead of "crucify". But that is not how writing works. The words come. The writer records. I also have discovered, through years of prayer, study and conversation, that many still are persecuted for doing nothing wrong. I find that horrifying. My teacher, however, was crucified for only doing good. He has taught me that truly bad things can happen to good people.

THE MESSAGE OF THE CROSS

With patience
Come the lessons
Of the ages.

They are not hard
Nor are we barred
From knowing.

The truth is plain
To see
If we but remove
The scales
From our eyes.

It is only we
Who build the walls
To hide the light.

The fears
Of the night
We gladly embrace
As we shield
Our eyes
From His Radiant Face.

The message of the cross
Is true:
You can still love
All those
Who crucify you.

HE SHOWED US HOW

At the beginning
Of His Ministry
He told us
To love
Our enemies.

At the end
Of His Ministry
He showed us how.

CONCLUSION

THE IMPETUS

To survive
Is such an effort;
To move forward
Takes such strain.

To do for others
Is not always easy,
Nor accepted
In the proper vein.

But a smile
From our Father
Provides the impetus
To proceed;
Where help
Is required
And we see a need.

MY STRENGTH

My strength
Is in the Lord
Who made
Heaven and earth
And small children;
Who made
The ocean
And minnow,
The mountain
And day lily,
The forest
And firefly,
The desert
And cactus flower;
Who loves
The everlasting

And fleeting,
The strong
And weak,
The large
And small;
Who Loves us all.

While I was doing some ordinary plumbing work, on our first house, many years ago, I ran into some problems. This was before the internet and thousands of videos of how to fix things. So, I called my dad; and explained how the guy at the plumbing store had told me to make this straightforward repair. It sounded so easy to me; yet I was having a really hard time with the plumbing repair. My dad's answer was, "It may sound simple, but it's never easy." I remember my dad's answer as if he told me yesterday; and not fifty years ago.

Though simply stated, loving our neighbor is not always easy. Loving our siblings is not always easy. It is not easy for them to love us either. Some of our neighbors are born in the city. Some are born in the country; maybe even the wilderness. Our neighbors are born of different shades and hues. Our neighbors are born in every corner of the world. Our neighbors are born of many religions; even no religion or beliefs. Our neighbors come from different backgrounds, with different gifts to share. To say that we are all the same would be inaccurate. To say that we are equal is truth.

Nan and I have three sons. They are not the same. They have different interests. They have different skills. They have different gifts to give. Each has given us concern from time to time. Each has needed us at different times in different ways. We have watched them grow; and have tried to give them what they need when they needed it. They did not always get what they wanted; no matter how hard they tried. Though they are not the same, we love them equally. That is what parents do. Just imagine how much Love a Perfect Parent might Give.

Our grandchildren call Nan by different names; some call her NanNa, some Nammi, some Nina. Those names stem from the oldest grandchild of each of our three sons as they first spoke Nan's name. Nan responds to all three names. She knows which family is speaking to her by the name for which she is called. Nan loves all of our grandchildren. It doesn't matter which name for her is used.

If we are to have Peace on Earth, that Peace that passeth all understanding, then we must begin by loving all of our neighbors, our siblings; and granting them the respect they deserve. For they deserve our respect simply for surviving the journeys that have brought them this far.

No one chooses their time or place of birth. No one chooses their starting place for their journey. Depending on how and where their start, everyone has a different path for their journey. It is so much better to cheer them on while they journey forth than to throw rocks at them and place briars along their path.

As in the wildflowers and symphonies, always remember that it is our blend that gives us beauty; it is our blend that makes us outstanding.

BONUS

POEMS AND MESSAGES

FROM 2016 - 2020

As a bonus I have included some of my poems and messages from 2016 through 2020. These are poems and messages that I posted, previously, on my website or on Google+.

I began posting weekly poems and messages on my website back in 2012. I kind of dropped my website, back in 2014, when Google+ came around. I found that Google+ had a larger audience; and that I could reach more poets. I actually virtually met a few really good poets from 2014 until Google+ closed its doors.

Some of the poems and messages, that follow, reiterate and expand some of the poems found earlier in my book. Others are new. I have published some of these poems and messages in other works. The poems and messages from 2019 and 2020 have never seen the light of day until now. I have included the dates that these were posted along with each title.

These are mostly poems and messages about my faith in my Lord and His Love for all of His children. If you do not want to read about my faith, then please stop here. They also expand on my beliefs, my family and my life.

I have not edited any of these works. They appear as they first appeared in my postings. I wrote these as a train-of-thought. Please disregard my grammatical efforts and try to see the meaning for what I intended.

If you proceed, please enjoy.

HER LOVE IS TRUE – January 2016

By many names
She is called.

Though many names,
She loves them all.

Each name special;
Coined anew.

Each name special;
Love shines through.

She sees each child;
Their love in bloom.

She loves each child
Her love is true.

Whatever name
Each child
Does use,
Her love
For them
Shines through
And through.

Our youngest son and his bride gave us a wonderful house warming present this past Thanksgiving. They gave us a stand-alone ornament . . . not one for the Christmas tree . . . but one for the shelf . . . or, as we have displayed, for our dining room table. It is a beautiful ornament with a snow man and snow woman surrounded by many packages. On each package (or gift) is the name of one of our family . . . eleven grandchildren . . . three sons . . . three daughters-in-law . . . seventeen wonderful children of all ages. On the snow man was my name . . . Pop Pop. On the snow woman was Nan's name . . . Nammi . . . the name Nan is called by our youngest son's four children.

Now . . . Nan is known by three different names . . . each coined by the first child of each son and daughter-in law. Our oldest son's children call Nan, NanNa. Our middle son's children call Nan, Nina. Our eleven grandchildren call Nan three different names. Each family is pretty consistent. Occasionally there is some confusion . . . however . . . Nan knows . . . when a grandchild calls her name . . . to which family that child belongs.

On the Tuesday before Christmas, the schools here let out a little early for the Christmas break. Our youngest grandchild, who is in pre-K, needed someone to watch him . . . since his mom teaches . . . and had to stay at school till the end of the day. Nan and I gladly volunteered to watch him. We had a wonderful afternoon . . . full of school stories and laughter. We had the honor of keeping him until after dinner.

At the dinner table, our youngest grandson noticed the Christmas ornament his aunt and uncle had given us. More importantly, he noticed the name "Nammi" written on the snow woman . . . the snow woman who represented Nan . . . the snow woman who represented the matriarch of the family. He asked Nan, "Why is Nammi written as your name?". Nan responded that that is the name she is called by his aunt and uncle's children. He then responded, "But your name is Nina." To which Nan responded, "I am known by three names . . . NanNa, Nammi and Nina." Then, Nan said, "I love all of the names you call me . . . and I love all of you."

I sat there . . . watching the proceedings described above . . . this poet . . . who loves metaphors and analogies . . . who is always searching for words to write of His Love . . . always searching for connections . . . always searching for His Messages. I sat there . . . and thought Wow . . . His Heavenly Hosts have handed me an easy one . . . not one everyone will want to hear . . . but a stunning lesson nonetheless.

I love it when the Peace, which passeth all understanding, flows through me. I love it when others . . . especially children . . . teach me a new lesson . . . or reinforce those lessons so precious to me. I love it when I can restate my beliefs in different ways . . . in ways that may reach a fresh ear . . . though I know what I believe may cause someone else to close their ear to my thoughts. I love it when He answers my

prayers . . . for wisdom . . . for patience . . . for understanding . . . for
His Love.

I love listening to the messages between mother and child . . . between
grandmother and grandchild. I love experiencing the growth of a
young person's mind . . . a young person growing in Love and Truth.

By many Names He is called . . . and, through all those names, He
Loves us all.

HE LOVES EACH ONE – July 2016

We all point
At each other
As if there's one
To blame;
But
We are all
In this world
Together;
And He Loves each one
The same.

Some of my organized religion brethren will disagree; but I believe . . .
I sincerely believe . . . that our Father, in Heaven, Loves each and
every one of us . . . and He Loves each and every one of us the same.
My Lord said, "The Father is no respecter of persons" . . . so . . . if we
think we have an edge . . . well . . . I don't think so.

For those with children . . . especially more than one child . . . I would
hope you will agree with me . . . that parents love each child equally.
That's not to say that one child might not need more at any one time
than another child . . . one might need a new winter coat . . . one might
need new shoes . . . one might need more help with their homework . . .
or going to baseball practice . . . or going to band practice . . . one
might be sick . . . one might really need a hug. We give to our children
depending on their needs . . . not necessarily depending on their wants.

What about the child that says, at some point, I hate you . . . or I don't
love you anymore . . . or leave me alone . . . or I'm old enough to think

for myself . . . or I don't want to live with you anymore? Do we not still love this child . . . much like the father of the prodigal son. We might be hurt . . . we might be disappointed . . . but we do not love any less.

Nan and I have raised three sons . . . well . . . Nan has done most of the work . . . our sons and their wives are now raising our eleven grandchildren . . . they love their children . . . and tend to their needs . . . as we loved them . . . and as we did the best we could to give them what they needed . . . when they needed . . . equally. I'll never say our sons, from time to time, never gave us a hard time . . . but I can say that we loved our sons deeply . . . in good times and in hard times . . . we never loved them less . . . and we loved each son equally.

I believe our Heavenly Father Loves in a similar manner . . . I'm not saying that because I think He is created in our image . . . it is just that I believe, in all my heart, that we have been Created in His . . . and I think my love for my children operates in accordance with His Love . . . though, of course, His Love is Perfect.

I would like to think that at some time . . . in the future . . . we could get it into our heads that the person we dislike . . . that we can't get along with . . . that we cannot . . . or will not trust . . . that that person is a child of the Most-High God. Why else would my Lord use a Samaritan as an example of a neighbor when He was speaking to the Jewish community? The Jews disliked the Samaritans . . . maybe hate is a better word . . . and they certainly didn't trust them . . . and my Lord knew that . . . that's why He Told the story as He Did.

We don't have to like all of our neighbors . . . and I doubt whether we will always trust them. But . . . we have to love them . . . they are our Father's children . . . and He Loves them every bit as much as He Loves us. My Lord summed up the law with two directives . . . love the Lord, your God, with all of your heart, mind, soul and strength . . . and love your neighbor as yourself . . . you know . . . even the one you don't like. He could not have been more clear. Let's get on with it.

What
Can I do
To serve You
Today?

Your children?
Their children?
In what form
Or way?

Which words
Do I write
To give them
Your Sight?

What sentence
Will rise
To give them
New Height?

I fight
For a way
To translate
What You Say.

Please help me
To give them
A better
Today.

I wrestle with how to help my Father's children all of the time . . . my quest has been with me for several decades . . . unfortunately, for me, this is one job from which I cannot retire.

It is never my intent, as I write, to mess with the beliefs of an individual. If someone believes . . . has faith . . . then I want them to continue . . . I wish to lead no one away from what they believe . . . I

only wish to lead those who can't . . . or won't believe . . . to His Feet . .
.

I spent much of a decade of my life pouring over religious materials . .
. books on religion . . . the Crusades . . . life in the early days of The
Way . . . life in and around the formation of early Christianity. I read
the Bible . . . cover to cover . . . several different versions . . . my
favorite still being the King James Version . . . the very Bible that I
received at Christmas . . . in 1958 . . . as I was being confirmed as a
member of our local church.

I remember, quite distinctly, being very confused as I started my
journey . . . a journey my mind formed around saving our young
nephew, Michael . . . I wanted so much to better understand . . . my
prayers for wisdom had been ongoing since the mid-1950s . . . then . . .
maybe thirty years later . . . I wanted more . . . an understanding of
how to make my life . . . Michael's life . . . the lives of His children . . .
more joyful . . . more loving . . . more forgiving . . . abler to withstand
the disappointments of life.

I have been told, by some, that there is a difference between the Old
Testament and the New Testament God because God Changed His
Mind about we, the human race . . . and that . . . with my Lord's birth . .
. God became a Loving God . . . and not a Wrathful God. I have been
told, by some, that there is no difference between the God of the Old
Testament and the God of the New Testament . . . that the Book of
Revelation proves, beyond a doubt, that our God is still a Wrathful
God . . . a Revengeful God.

My studies . . . my prayers . . . my internal conversations with my Lord
have cast a different light on the subject of our Heavenly Father. My
conclusion is that God is Changeless . . . it is we who have grown . . .
and have changed the way we look at Him. When we are young, we
fear our parents . . . at least I did. As we grow older, we learn to love
our parents as friends . . . as the pinnacle of wisdom and truth . . . as
our support system . . . as our mentors . . . we do for them because we
love them . . . not because we fear them.

As I read . . . and reread the Old Testament, I began to see a difference
in the way the later prophets saw our Father . . . they saw Him as a

more Loving Father . . . a Father Who Looked for our hearts . . . and our love . . . instead of our sacrifices . . . and our fear. Then . . . of course . . . my Lord came down from His Throne . . . to be the Son of man . . . in addition to His Rightful Title of Son of God.

My Lord Taught a Loving Father . . . a Father Who Searches for all of His lost children . . . and Rejoices when they return . . . a Father of Forgiveness . . . and Tender Mercies . . . a Father Who Would Send His Son to Teach us . . . and Guide us . . . and Live among us . . . Die for us so that we would live . . . and Become One with us through His Spirit of Truth . . . whether we recognize Him . . . or not.

I learned . . . and continue to learn . . . how much our Father Loves us . . . how my Lord continues to Teach me about my Father . . . and His Love . . . and His Forgiveness . . . how my Lord brings me Joy . . . when all is falling around me . . . how He picks me up when I fall . . . how He Walks beside me when I feel alone . . . how He Prepares a Place for me in His Mansion Home.

I have such Joy from my Lord . . . and our Father . . . I do for my God . . . the Most-High God . . . out of Love . . . out of Respect . . . out of my consciousness of His Presence in my life.

I now know one thing that is certain . . . not simply a belief . . . but knowledge . . . and that is that my Father . . . our Father . . . Loves me more than I can express in words . . . His Love Overwhelms me.

I would simply love to find the words to bring all of my brothers and sisters to this Joy of His Salvation . . . His Peace that passeth all understanding . . . His Love . . . which Has No Limits.

How I would love to give my brothers and sisters a better today.

SHOW YOUR LIGHT – September 2016

Please, Lord,
Protect my siblings
In Ways
Unknown.

Please
Let them see
How in You
We've grown.

Hold them each
In Your Loving Arms.

Protect them please
From all earthly harms.

Please, Lord,
Walk with them
Though
They may not know.

Watch their path
Wherever
They may go.

Bring them home
When they lose their way.

Show Your Light
Throughout their day.

Please, Lord,
Place Your Hand
On
Their fevered head.

Sit with them
When
They're full of dread.

Hold their hand
When
They won't get up.

Cry with them

When
They drink of Your Cup.

Please, Lord,
Bless my siblings;
This I pray:
Show Your Light
While they walk
In gray.

I've never been big on public prayer. My Lord said for us to go off by ourselves . . . and pray to our Father in private . . . I tend to listen to the Word . . . I believe it is we, individually, who need to build a relationship with the Most-High God. He did teach us one Prayer . . . after His Disciples asked over and over again . . . a Prayer to our Father in Heaven . . . a prayer we can all say privately . . . or publicly.

Not to say I don't believe in public prayer . . . there is comfort in it . . . it teaches others how to pray . . . and I believe our Lord . . . and His Heavenly Hosts . . . Hear all prayers . . . it's just that I'm an introvert . . . so I'm the one who goes off by himself to pray.

As many who are impacted . . . who hear the prayers of others . . . I believe there are many more who never hear our prayers . . . may never know they are being prayed for . . . and this is my prayer for them . . . those who do not know . . . those who are still children of the Most-High God . . . but have never been introduced to Him . . . or have a hard time believing in a Father Who Cares . . . Who Loves them . . . Who Forgives them of their sins.

As a parent, I love my children and grandchildren . . . even when I don't see them so often. Some are in their teenage years . . . those years of independence . . . breaking away. At some time . . . they will probably get bored with their Pop Pop . . . but I will love them just the same. Parents . . . who never see their kids . . . still love them. Parents . . . whose kids have drifted away . . . still love their children. Parents . . . who give their children up for adoption . . . still love their children. At least . . . I think most parents continue to love their children . . . whether their children love them or not.

We are made in His Image . . . and I believe we love as He Does . . . though not as much . . . though not as greatly . . . though not as forgiving . . . but we do love our children. So . . . I believe He Loves His children . . . even more than we love ours . . . and that He Even Loves His children who do not know Him . . . or do not believe in Him . . . or are confused as to Who He Really Is.

As I sat down this week to write, the poem above shouted forth . . . a prayer for all of those who do not know my Lord as I do. Now . . . I do not know all of the needs of my siblings . . . but He Does . . . and that is all that is truly important . . . so I ask Him to protect my siblings in ways unknown to me . . . and to be with my siblings no matter what they are going through . . . He Knows their needs . . . I don't need to . . . I just need to ask His Presence in their lives . . . I just need to shed a tear for them . . . for whatever they are going through . . . I just need to say . . . out loud . . . that I am their brother . . . and I want them to know Him as I do . . . to feel His Presence . . . even if they do not know the Significance of Who they feel.

I share this prayer with all . . . it is a prayer anyone can say aloud . . . it is a prayer for sister and brother . . . it is prayer . . . for those who know Him . . . to share with those who don't.

Dear Lord, Hold them each in Your Loving Arms . . . Protect them please from all earthly harms.

IT'S OK TO STAY – October 2016

Father,
Give me peace,
I pray.

See me through
Each day.

Right me
When I fall.

Help me love
Them all.

Give me patience,
Lord.

Cling me to
Your Word.

Let me drift
Not much.

Help me search
Your Touch.

When I lose
My way,
Grab my hand
And Say,
It's OK
To stay
By Your Side.

Last week I shared a prayer to and for all of my brothers and
sisters. This week I share a prayer for me . . . and maybe you can use it
for yourself.

I have always thought it wise when the airline stewards tell the
passengers to mask themselves . . . before they tend to anyone else. It's
best, I think, to be at your best before you try to help someone else . . .
so I may have been off the mark by posting a prayer for others . . .
before a prayer for myself . . . but poems come to me in whatever order
they wish . . . and I do my best to do their bidding.

I have made so many mistakes in my life . . . and when I've made one .
. . I always seek Him first . . . those closest to me either prefer to
criticize me . . . or they tell me it's OK . . . but . . . when I know it's not
OK . . . I go to Him . . . and rest by His Side . . . I always want to be by
His Side . . . He Loves me for who I am . . . He Does Not Make Light
of my trials. His Forgiveness . . . when I repent . . . is Overwhelming.

85

Help me love them all is crucial to me . . . so important in my prayer life . . . to me . . . it's pretty easy to love my Lord with all of my heart, mind, soul and strength . . . not so easy to love my brothers and sisters . . . the children of our Father . . . I want to . . . but it is so hard sometimes . . . I believe that is why my Lord stressed those two commandments . . . He Knew if we could love our neighbors as ourselves . . . we could get along . . . so important to the coming of Heaven on earth . . . so important to peace on earth . . . good will toward all mankind.

Cling me to Your Word . . . I need so much to center myself in Him . . . and His Word . . . not to the words of others . . . not to the words of some who believe they are smarter . . . or wiser . . . than He Who is my Father . . . in He Who is my Lord . . . let me cling to Your Word, my Lord . . . let me go Your Way . . . let me love Your Children . . . let me know Your Will . . . for it is only with Your Word that the Universe seems Right.

See me through each day is a prayer I've been saying for as long as I can remember . . . it is another essential . . . it is like getting dressed in the morning . . . getting prepared to face the day. Without Him . . . I can't face the day . . . He is my Strength . . . He is my Patience . . . He is my Love . . . He is All to me . . . He Has Seen me through all of my trials and tribulations . . . my mistakes . . . my victories . . . without Him, I am nothing . . . please see me through each day . . . and He Has.

I always want Him to know I know He is my Lord . . . and yes . . . He Knows . . . He Is God . . . but I want Him to know I know . . . like the young college student . . . who stood up in church last Sunday to thank her mom . . . who just happened to be sitting next to her . . . for she wanted her mom to know how much she loved her . . . and appreciated all that she had done for her . . . that's what I want for Him to Hear . . . from my heart . . . that I know Who He Is . . . and what He Has Done for me.

I love Him so . . . and need . . . so much . . . to stay by His Side.

LET YOUR LIGHT – November 2016

Father,
In all
That I do,
Help me
To point them all
To You.

Let my words
Be true
In what I say
For You.

Let my words
See through
What we mean
To You.

Help me shout
What You're About.

Let my joy
Ring through for You.

Let Your Light
Shine through
These words;
Let Your Love
For us
Be Heard.

I promised my Lord . . . back in the 1980s . . . standing on the rock . . . which I refer to as my Gethsemane . . . that I would write for Him . . . and teach about Him . . . for as long as I could hold a pen . . . and speak with clarity. I actually tried to make a deal . . . He Would Heal our nephew, Michael . . . and I would write and teach . . . but Michael was taken from us . . . though He Was Taken Home . . . by a Loving Father. I wrote . . . not long after . . . that one can make no deals with God . . . it is His Will . . . not ours . . . that will be done. I will never

have the necessary intellect to understand or question His Will. So . . .
I will fulfill my promise to Him . . . I will write for Him . . . and I will
teach His Love . . . His Forgiveness . . . His Tender Mercies . . . as long
as He Allows.

I say these words because I have received some helpful, meaningful
words from family and friends . . . that I should be paid for being an
author . . . that . . . for some reason . . . my words should not come
cheap. I have been informed, by some, that I should charge more for
my books on Kindle . . . my paperbacks on Amazon . . . that it appears
that my books are worthless . . . because they are so cheap. But . . . my
Lord has blessed me . . . with gifts of Love . . . but also with pensions
that allow me to pay a mortgage . . . a roof over Nan's and my heads . .
. food on the table . . . a car in the garage . . . and a week's vacation for
our entire family. Money is not something for which I write . . . I write
for Him . . . in the hope that you will find Him too . . . and know His
Joy.

I believe poets should have a passion for something . . . truth . . .
beauty . . . love . . . peace . . . change . . . unfairness . . . social injustice
. . . nature . . . something that is missing in the lexicon . . . something
that spurs thought . . . and conversation. I believe poets hold some
candle . . . lit so that it can be seen . . . from a distance . . . over time . .
. not that the poet should be seen . . . but that their light should be seen
. . . it is enough that the light is seen . . . recognition of the author only
muddies the discourse. My passion is the Love of our Heavenly Father
. . . His Love for me . . . His Love for all of His children . . . my
siblings. Though I can never be as passionate as Him . . . for He sent
His Only Son to Introduce us to Him . . . to Teach His Love . . . His
Forgiveness . . . His Tender Mercies . . . and we did not see Him for
Who He Was and Is . . . His Own Son . . . Who Laid Down His Life
for us . . . so that all of us . . . whether we know Him or not . . . would
have His Spirit Reside within us . . . to Guide us . . . and to Deliver us
Home . . . if only we see His Light. That is my passion . . . to point
others . . . my siblings . . . to His Light.

My Lord sent His Disciples out two by two . . . He paired them
because loneliness is even more difficult when we have to face a
confused or angry crowd. He also told them that their work was
worthy of pay . . . that they should have a roof over their head . . .

maybe provided by someone else . . . and they should have food to eat . . . maybe provided by someone else . . . in other words . . . if they were working for Him . . . they would be provided for . . . they need not worry about shelter or food.

My Lord Has Blessed me with shelter . . . and food . . . and family . . . a place to rest my head . . . a place not to hunger . . . a place of love . . . and a sense of Love . . . those are all I need to continue my work . . . those are all I need to complete my promise . . . decades later . . . I never tire of serving Him . . . and His children.

I enjoy giving away my thoughts . . . I enjoy sharing with His children that which can bring them Joy . . . I wish for others to see my candle burning for Him . . . my insignificant light, shining in the distance, allowing others to see His Significance . . . I want others to know a little of what I know . . . so that they can expand what little I know . . . so that they can someday light a bonfire of Love.

Let Your Light/Shine through/These words; Let Your Love/For us/Be heard.

LET MY THOUGHTS – January 2017

Father,
Help me do for You
Without
Thinking of me.

Let my thoughts
Be about You
And Your children
As I sit and write
With Your Spirit.

Let my ego dissolve
As I resolve myself
In You.

Let my cares
Remain inside

As I abide
In Your Love.

I need no thoughts
Of me to be
As I search through
These words I see.

Please see me through
All I'm to do.

Please take my ego
And place behind
My love for You;
And thoughts sublime
For your children.

Sometimes it's difficult to see past the downcast eyes of the introverted artist into the towering ego that resides inside . . . whether the artist acts . . . or paints . . . or writes . . . whether they write words or compose music . . . whether the artist sings . . . or dances . . . or crochets . . . or quilts . . . or whatever the artist sees as their talent . . . or gift. For . . . whatever it is that an artist performs . . . they usually want some attention . . . from an audience . . . while they are performing . . . and when their performance is over . . . whether that performance is of any value to the particular audience or not.

I gave up watching award shows long ago . . . but it's hard to read any news . . . or watch any news without the artists . . . who are in attendance at these award shows . . . showing up . . . with their wonderful gowns . . . and tuxedos . . . with their wonderful speeches of thanks . . . or political leanings . . . and their congratulations of self . . . and fellow artists . . . for all the wonderful things that they are doing for humanity. There are so many award programs . . . for theater . . . for the cinema . . . for TV . . . for music . . . of all kinds . . . it is hard to go through a month without one being advertised . . . then being discussed for the beauty of the gowns . . . for the beauty of the artists . . . for the wonder of the causes.

I know . . . I know . . . this is just the world . . . loving itself . . . as it has for most of recorded history . . . I need to get over it . . . and appreciate what these individuals are actually doing for His children . . . I need to get the log out of my own eye . . . before I look for the sliver in theirs . . . I get it.

But it bothers me . . . continuously bothers me . . . that . . . in my being . . . I look for approval . . . and praise also. I can't get around it . . . from my first manuscript . . . some thirty years ago . . . I've been looking for approval . . . and am usually disappointed when none is received . . . whether from publishers . . . or family . . . or friends . . . or uninterested parties . . . even though I know I only need please my Lord . . . there is an ego . . . inside of me . . . that looks for more.

In Matthew, Chapter 6, my Lord speaks of giving. In verses 2-4, my Lord begins; "Therefore when thou doest thine alms, do not sound the trumpet before thee, as the hypocrites do in the synagogues and in the streets, that they may have glory of men. Verily I say to you, they have their reward. But when thou doest alms, let not thy left hand know what thy right hand doeth: That thy alms may be in secret: and thy Father which seeth in secret shall reward thee openly." (KJV)

I wrestle with this passage of Matthew a lot . . . I have been given gifts . . . and I need to return them to His children . . . without looking for anything in return . . . I need give . . . with my writing hand . . . without knowing what those gifts will bring . . . for if I look for accolades . . . from my peers . . . from my family . . . from my friends . . . from those who may partake of my gifts . . . than those accolades will be my reward . . . and that might be all. However . . . if I look for nothing . . . if I simply give . . . to any and all . . . then . . . my Lord promises . . . our Father will reward me openly . . . the greatest reward I could ever receive . . . His Salvation . . . His Love . . . His Forgiveness . . . His Tender Mercies . . . in whatever ways He Sees Fit . . . not what I want . . . . but what He Wants for me.

So . . . I believe . . . it is intent . . . it is the why . . . it is the meaning . . . the motive . . . behind the act . . . the art . . . that is important . . . and I have to ask myself . . . would I write if no one else read my work? My answer is that I have . . . though . . . I must admit . . . in my first decade of writing poems . . . almost thirty years ago . . . I wrote to help myself

. . . every bit as much as praising my Lord. I know that now more than ever . . . for to write one's pain . . . along with writing His Presence . . . in getting through the pain . . . well . . . it has a dual purpose . . . healing . . . and understanding Who Is Healing. For now . . . I simply love Him so . . . and I want the world to know . . . whether the world is listening . . . or not.

Let my ego dissolve/As I resolve myself/In You.

TO JUDGE – March 2017

He Taught:
Let he
Who is
Without sin
Cast
The first stone;
Also
Remove
The beam
From
Your own eye
Before
You look
For the sliver
In
Another's eye.

Why
Do we need
To judge;
You and I?

Why
Would we test
Our Teacher?

I'm having a difficult time finding any live shows to watch nowadays . . . so many so full of criticism . . . so many wanting to stir the pot . . . or take a bat to the beehive . . . so many negative comments about pretty much anything and everything . . . I dislike discussing anything being delivered on the news . . . where there are only a few minutes devoted to any good news stories at the end of the broadcasts.

My Webster's New World College Dictionary (yes . . . I still use a dictionary) defines gospel as a good story . . . and good news . . . probably the reason for a Bible entitled the Good News Bible. I wonder why those who wrote and translated the original Greek . . . thought this was good news. I mean . . . there is some horrific stories in it . . . some real drama . . . a beheading of a wonderful, principled individual . . . devoted to introducing his followers to the King of kings . . . then the awful death of a sinless individual . . . the Son of God . . . the Son of man . . . I mean there is so much bad news in the Gospel . . . treachery . . . lying . . . traitorous villains . . . denial . . . and death . . . lots of death . . . even to innocent children . . . why on earth would we think this is good news?

And the time in which this good news took place . . . a time of Roman authority . . . and though the Roman State may have been all powerful at the time . . . yet the leadership was ruthless . . . feeding people to the lions . . . having fun watching individuals fight to the death . . . even burning the Word's followers as torches at parties. This was not a good time . . . though it may have been the most peaceful time on the planet thus far . . . at least there was rule of law . . . and commerce . . . maybe this was the best time for my Lord to come . . . for the Word to spread the Word . . . so that there would be some Good News . . . to get people through the difficult times . . . then . . . and in the future.

Nan and I were in high school in the early 1960s . . . when John F. Kennedy was assassinated . . . then Robert Kennedy . . . I was in college in the late 1960s . . . when Martin Luther King was assassinated . . . and the Democratic Convention in Chicago . . . during the Vietnam War . . . during the riots on college campuses . . . including the one on which I attended . . . it was an awful time . . . riots in the street . . . social injustice . . . hatred of the military . . . disrespect for those returning from war . . . but Nan and I were in love . . . we were high school sweethearts . . . we were engaged in 1966 . . . married in 1967 . . . while I was still in school . . . our oldest son was born in 1969 . . . Nan and I were so busy . . . we seldom even watched the news . . . which was only maybe a half hour back then . . . we were so busy . . . and happy . . . and full of good news . . . that that horrible decade passed over us . . . like a dark cloud . . . only later . . . when I looked at a Time Magazine capture of the 1960s . . . did I realize how awful it was.

That's one of the truly significant aspects of the Good News . . . understanding that we can deal with terrible, awful, distasteful, hateful stuff . . . if we are at peace inside . . . if we are positive about our love for each other . . . if we are in love with our Father in Heaven . . . if we can follow those two wonderful commandment . . . loving Him with all we got . . . loving others as ourselves . . . we can get through whatever the hateful elements are that we may know . . . or may not know . . . that surround us . . . that are the world.

Sometimes . . . we have to make our own good news . . . look at our blessings . . . and if we feel we have no blessings . . . then we have to be a blessing to someone else . . . then open our hearts to the blessings that service to each other brings.

I also believe we need to spend less time judging . . . and more time living . . . and maybe even more time loving . . . like all of those songs of the 1960s . . . loving each other . . . free love in the Godliest context . . . love . . . forgiveness . . . tender mercies.

And . . . finally . . . I believe we need to look at ourselves first . . . before we judge another . . . we are not perfect . . . how can we expect someone else to be? And . . . we need be careful about throwing stones . . . insults . . . judgments . . . at others . . . unless we are perfect . . . and . . . trust me . . . we are not . . . only One Was . . . and it is His Words I quote . . . it is His Teachings I want to follow . . . not the world's . . . not those who believe it is appropriate to judge . . . and make fun of . . . others.

I have often said . . . I may not condone another's actions . . . but I cannot judge them . . . their worth . . . their motives . . . their lives . . . I have not been where they have been . . . I may not like what I'm seeing . . . but I am not their Judge . . . Only One Can Judge . . . that is not my job . . . that is His . . . my Teacher . . . my Lord.

IT IS TIME – June 2017

Why the hatred?

Do we truly believe
We are better
Than
Our brothers and sisters?

Do we truly believe
We know better
Than those
Who stand among us?

What do we prove
By destroying another;
By our words
Or actions?

Our Father
Is no respecter of persons;
He Loves each of us
The same;
It matters not
The color of our skin,
Or our sex,
Or our nationality,
Or our religion.

Why the hatred?

The rain falls
On the just and unjust.

No one is better
Than another.

Though we may think
Differently;
And look

Differently;
And speak
Differently;
And act
Differently;
His Spirit Indwells us all.

It is time
To remove our blinders;
And see His children
As He Sees them;
With Love,
And Compassion,
And Forgiveness,
And Tender Mercies.

I don't get it . . . I just don't get it.

I read . . . long ago . . . that there are two things which will forever
want to separate us . . . nationality . . . and religion . . . but . . . I think
there may be more.

I understand . . . on the surface . . . the distinction of nations . . . the
sovereignty of nations . . . I get caught up in my own pride of country .
. . tears still well in my eyes when I hear our anthem . . . so . . . I get it .
. . and I get it when I watch the individual and team battles of an
Olympics . . . though I do not get a battle of nations . . . for the sake of
winning a citizenry to another way of thinking . . . of believing . . . of
living.

But . . . the battles over religion just don't make sense to me at
all. Religion . . . to me . . . is my relationship with my . . . our . . .
Heavenly Father. Organized religion attempts to tell me how and what
I should believe . . . but . . . religion is mine to own . . . no one can tell
me what He means to me . . . no one. Though my Lutheran upbringing
may have brought stories to my ears . . . it was His Spirit . . . inside of
me . . . Who made those stories come alive . . . and separated the wheat
from the chaff. Why would anyone fight about their relationship with
the Most High God . . . the I AM?

I cannot make another believe as I do . . . I can paint pictures . . . I can write poetry . . . I can lead by example . . . through kindness . . . and love . . . but I can't make others believe . . . it doesn't work that way . . . my Lord is my Light . . . and I can do my best to lead others to His Light . . . but they may not wish to follow . . . or they may be blinded . . . either way . . . others simply may not see as I do . . . and destroying them with my judgment or my sword will not help them to see any better.

Hatred solves nothing . . . it is like a cancer . . . multiplying itself as it hides under our skin . . . killing the very cells of kindness . . . killing the very cells of love . . . killing the very cells of forgiveness . . . it eats away . . . it destroys our happiness . . . hatred is of no value to anyone. My Lord hated no one . . . He Forgave even those who nailed Him to the cross . . . He Loved even those who had not a clue as to Who He Was . . . He Loves even those who have not a clue as to Who He Is.

I don't get it . . . I just don't get it.

We are born of different colors of skin . . . we are born in different places around the globe . . . we do not choose the color of our skin . . . we do not choose our place of birth . . . we do not choose what our family and teachers teach us about the world . . . we do not choose what our family and teachers teach us about our Father . . . even if they teach us anything about our Father at all. We cannot help it if some tragedy befalls those who came before us . . . and they have turned from their belief . . . we cannot help what has come before . . . and we cannot help the path that lies before us . . . though . . . we can certainly defy our path . . . and go another way. But . . . no matter our color of skin . . . no matter our place of birth . . . His Spirit of Truth . . . The Comforter . . . Resides inside each of us . . . He Is our Guide . . . He Is our Light . . . no matter from where we begin . . . no matter what path has been chosen by our family and friends . . . no matter what path we decide to take.

Instead of looking at our brothers and sisters from our frame of reference . . . from our color of skin . . . from our sex . . . from our place of birth . . . and all of the implications that go with our state of being . . . why not look at our brothers and sisters from our Father's

Frame of Reference . . . as the Parent of all . . . with the Knowledge that all who walk with us . . . no matter what they look like . . . no matter where they were born . . . that The Parent Loves all . . . Forgives all . . . and Showers His Tender Mercies on all.

I know . . . I know . . . so few will listen to my voice . . . to the Love He Has Placed on my heart . . . and those who agree . . . have . . . most likely . . . already agreed.

I just have to say I don't get it . . . I just don't get it.

Why can't we just agree to disagree? We are not the same . . . we will never be the same . . . our backgrounds are not the same . . . our languages are not the same . . . our places of birth are not the same . . . we do not look the same . . . the families we grew up with are not the same . . . the neighborhoods in which we grew are not the same . . . the schools in which we attended . . . and the teachers who taught us are not the same . . . so . . . why in the world would we expect everyone else to think the same?

It is time/To remove our blinders/And see His children/As He Sees them/With Love/And Compassion/And Forgiveness/And Tender Mercies.

TEARS – September 2017

Father,
Hear their prayers;
Hear their pleads;
Be with them
As they search
Their needs.

Be their strength;
Be their peace;
Be there
As they release
Their fears
And tears.

Though they feel
They are
On sinking sand,
Lift them
With
Your Steadfast Hand.

Hold them in
Your Loving Arms;
Soothe them with
Your Loving Grace;
Show them
Your Sorrow;
Tears Flowing Down
Your Loving Face.

Father,
Hear their prayers;
Calm their fears;
Be with them
As they wipe
Their tears.

Keep them from
All harm and pain;
Help them back
To You
Again.

It was only a week between the crowds gathering to watch the solar eclipse and Hurricane Harvey beating down the shores of Texas and Louisiana . . . a week between the glory of nature . . . and the destruction of nature . . . a week between the smiles and applause of hundreds of thousands as they gathered to witness science at its finest and the gasps and tears of hundreds of thousands as they lost mostly everything to science at its worst . . . yet a week of being together . . . no matter race . . . no matter creed . . . no matter nationality . . . hands helping hands . . . nature at its worst . . . humanity at its best.

Though I always do shed tears while watching neighbor risking life for neighbor . . . when I see a stranger hugging another stranger . . . after being saved . . . after being rescued . . . especially when a child is handed back to a parent . . . the tears shedding in the picture . . . the tears flowing down my cheek . . . the beauty of the human race helping each other . . . holding children . . . lifting wheel chairs . . . pulling boats . . . lifting into helicopters . . . arriving in the nick of time . . . tired . . . drained . . . yet continually moving . . . continually helping . . . continuing saving and serving brother and sister. I am not surprised . . . at the calling of men and women who help other men and women . . . I am not surprised . . . because deep down . . . I know we are all brothers and sisters . . . deep down . . . I know we have a Loving Parent . . . deep down . . . I know His Love is shared by all . . . even if all do not know or forget that we are His children.

On those occasions when our news stations show disasters occurring around the globe . . . I see other nations . . . other children . . . I see His children helping their brothers and sisters in the same way . . . though they may be of different races . . . different creeds . . . different nationalities . . . their duty to their friends . . . their neighbors . . . strangers . . . is the same . . . different continents . . . different countries . . . they rescue their sisters and brothers . . . even if they do not recognize them as such.

The human spirit is a mighty spirit because we are made in His Image. His Spirit is Infinite . . . and we share a small part of Him . . . His Spirit . . . and that small part is Mighty indeed.

The science of this earth is both beautiful and ugly . . . is awesome and awful . . . both fills and drains the soul. We can watch the wonder of the moon drifting between the earth and sun one day . . . and we can witness the destructive forces of a hurricane the next . . . it is all here . . . we all have to face it . . . and we can face it alone . . . or we can face it together . . . it is our choice.

I know there are many who witness the destructive forces of nature and swear there can be no God . . . that no Loving God would allow the death of so many . . . the destruction of so much . . . that a Loving God would place us on a loving planet . . . and would allow nothing to harm us . . . but . . . the science of a planet is what it is . . . a sphere of molten rock and metal . . . plates shifting on the currents of the molten rock . . . held in its elliptical path by the gravity of the sun . . . which heats certain parts . . . while other parts cool . . . creating winds . . . picking up waves . . . and balancing itself in whatever way . . . and sometimes . . . we . . . the human race . . . are in the way.

The earth . . . this planet . . . the place on which we live . . . will continue to act in whatever way it wishes . . . and I can do nothing about it. The people . . . who inhabit this earth . . . who care for it . . . and the other species who co-exist . . . are another matter. I have not read that His Spirit was Breathed onto the planet . . . only into the people . . . His children. It is we who are created in His Image. This planet may replicate a pattern . . . one that is kept in its place by the forces of the universe . . . but it is we . . . His Children . . . who have received His Spirit. There is no love . . . no forgiveness inherent in a planet . . . but Love and Forgiveness indwell our very souls.

My Lord was here . . . on earth . . . for a short while. I know not what weather patterns He experienced while here. I read that He did experience rough waters . . . I imagine He experience heat and cold . . . I know He experienced the death of loved ones . . . the beheading of a cousin . . . most likely the death of His earthly father . . . I still believe He Cried when He brought back His friend Lazarus . . . not because Lazarus had died . . . but because He Knew what Lazarus was going to face on this earth . . . after my Lord Ascended. For the earth can be a cruel place . . . especially when His children refuse to believe in His Spirit. I believe my Lord Knows our tribulations . . . I believe He Loves all of His children.

One Truth/I know/One Truth/That Flows/To the giving. My Lord Knows/The sorrows/Of the living.

I ASK MY LORD – September 2017

As I try
To rest,
To sleep,
I ask my Lord,
My troubles steep,
To grant me Peace;

To Help me swim
Through waters deep.

So tired,
And mired
In all
The pain,
I seek
To rise
And face
Again
The path
I can't see
To the end.

I try
To clear
My mind
To sleep;
But storms
Ignite
With clouds
So deep,
And thunder
Wrestles with
This weary head;
And fills it full
Of din
And dread.

Once more
I ask
My thoughts
To Take;
And Give
This head
A needed break;
To Bring
All siblings
Safely home;

Convince them
They are not alone.

I ask
For Peace;
I ask
Release;
I ask my Lord
This pain
To cease.

Another week . . . another prayer.

Last week Hurricane Harvey was beating on Texas . . . this week
Hurricane Irma is fast approaching Florida . . . and I wonder if anyone
affected . . . by any means . . . can get any rest. I find storms . . . of any
kind . . . at any place . . . rob us of our rest.

Natural disasters . . . for good or bad . . . tend to bring large portions of
a population together . . . those in the path of the approaching disaster .
. . pray to be spared . . . those not in the path . . . pray for the safety and
well-being of those who are . . . and many . . . so many . . . pitch in to
help their neighbors . . . neighbors they may . . . or may not know . . .
humanity is often strengthened . . . often comes together . . . when the
worst of nature comes our way.

But . . . the poem above . . . is not just about natural disasters . . . for
many face . . . to them . . . disasters . . . unbearable pain . . . in the
privacy of their own home . . . in the privacy of their own room . . . in
the privacy of their own being . . . the pain is within . . . and often no
one knows . . . except them . . . and the Lord.

I feel for all who are putting their lives back together after all of the
natural disasters . . . all over the world . . . for their losses . . . in loved
ones . . . in property . . . in memories . . . both the memories lost in the
disaster . . . and the memories they will forever have of their loss . . . I
have never had their exact experience . . . so I cannot . . . in good
conscience . . . say I know how they feel. But . . . I have lost loved
ones . . . mother . . . father . . . brother . . . friends . . . and a young
nephew . . . whose death changed my life. And I know the pain of

being alone . . . while surrounded by family and friends . . . there is pain . . . unbearable, unbelievable pain . . . disasters of self . . . that we bear . . . inside.

Though I have lived a good . . . and a fairly fruitful life . . . though I have made it through more than the Biblical three score and ten years . . . though I can look back at some successes . . . at a wonderful family . . . at a good friend and wife . . . of marriage fast approaching the fifty-year mark . . . yet . . . the scars are still here . . . I can still feel them trying to stretch to match the adjoining healthy skin . . . they still are with me . . . and they force me to feel for what my sisters and brothers are feeling . . . and so I pray for them . . . so that they may heal as I have . . . with my Lord as their Healer . . . with my Lord as their Teacher . . . with my Lord as their Lord.

There is a story . . . I am reminded of . . . as I write this morning . . . of my Lord . . . sleeping in the hull of a small boat . . . riding in the storm . . . on the water . . . the boat being beaten by the waves . . . large in proportion to the boat . . . His friends . . . His Disciples . . . were all afraid . . . they thought they were going to die . . . that the boat would be capsized . . . that they would be thrown into the troubled sea . . . but my Lord was asleep . . . He was resting . . . while His friends were afraid . . . for their lives . . . and so they awakened Him . . . from His sleep . . . from His rest . . . so that He would quell the storm. I . . . so much . . . want to be able to sleep . . . through the storms . . . I wish I did not have to call on His Name each time I face one . . . but I still do

And so . . . I lie awake at night . . . feeling for those who feel they have nothing . . . either from their loss from a natural disaster . . . or from their loss of self . . . their loss of confidence . . . their loss of loved ones . . . their experience of abuse . . . their loss of innocence . . . their loss of spirit . . . I pray for those who feel loneliness . . . who feel helplessness . . . who feel lost . . . for I was lost . . . and now I'm Found. I pray for all who have not Him to Quell their storms . . . their pain inside I cannot hide.

I ask/For Peace;/I ask/Release;/I ask my Lord/This pain/To cease.

JUST ONE – February 2018

What
Do I do
Today
To capture
A way
To spread
His Love?

What words
Can I choose
To support
A sister
Or brother?

How
Can I cast out
Any doubt
That we
Are not alone?

How
Can I convince
Just one
That we are all
Just one?

How
Can I describe
To all
That victory
Can be won
Once
We have begun
To work
Together?

My words
Always

Fall short;
Yet,
I will not
Abort
This task
To ask
That we love
His children;
Our siblings.

This has been a common theme for me over the decades . . . attempting to bring all of His children unto the realization that we are brothers and sisters . . . no matter our color or creed . . . no matter where we were born . . . or under what circumstances. We will never think alike . . . but we can love each other . . . we may never like all of our siblings . . . happens in many families . . . but we can still love them . . . and reconcile with them . . . because we are sisters and brothers. I am always reminded of the greatest commandment . . . love the Lord, your God, with all of your heart, mind, soul and strength . . . and love your neighbor as yourself . . . so easy to hear . . . so hard to accomplish.

If we could just work together . . . to accomplish some simple goals . . . like respecting each other . . . no matter our beliefs . . . no matter our nationalities . . . then . . . maybe . . . just maybe . . . we could find the space . . . and the time . . . to listen to one another . . . not shout at one another . . . but speak with one another . . . and listen to one another . . . until we can find that common ground that binds us all . . . until we can understand the reasons we believe as we do . . . until we can understand the cultures in which we were raised . . . until we can understand the hesitancy to listen . . . until we can understand the hesitancy to understand. No one wants to be wrong . . . and no one wants to hear that everything they have witnessed and believed are wrong. It makes no sense . . . to me . . . to try to prove a sister or brother wrong . . . when I might not have it perfectly right.

So . . . I continue in my task . . . to bring His children to the understanding that we are all His children . . . most likely an impossible task . . . for it is so hard to convince the righteous that others may be righteous too.

How/Can I convince/Just one/That we are all/Just one? How/Can I describe/To all/That victory/Can be won/Once/We have begun/To work/Together?

I don't know . . . but I will keep trying.

THE BEAUTY OF THE FABRIC – July 2018

Family
Is a fine thread
Woven
Through the fabric
Of time.

It is we
Who weave;
In colors muted
Or bright;
In shades dark
Or light;
Woven by day
Or by night.

When our thread
Finds its way
Through the fabric
Of His Way,
Beauty
Will display.

Though we
May control
The colors and shades
We repeat,
It is He
Who Designs
The Beauty of the Fabric
Complete.

Our family vacation is over for this year. Every year . . . for the past maybe fifteen . . . Nan and I have been taking the boys . . . their wives . . . and all of the grandchildren . . . away . . . for a week. We've told the boys that they are receiving their inheritance . . . one week . . . one year . . . at a time. They don't seem to mind.

We've gone to a couple different locations over the years. The houses have changed . . . since the family has gotten bigger. Nan and I have a budget . . . but we try to get the biggest house we can . . . with as many bedrooms and bathrooms as we can . . . since not only has the family gotten bigger . . . but older . . . and the older grandchildren prefer some privacy.

On one of our last evenings . . . this year . . . we were all able to congregate in the great room of our rental home . . . and sing songs . . . led by our oldest granddaughter on guitar. We sang some old standards . . . then some 70's and 80's rock . . . then some modern stuff . . . so we played across the generations . . . and no one seemed to mind . . . it was special . . . as is our family.

We spent a few hours at the Wright Memorial Museum at Kitty Hawk . . . this year . . . and marveled at the genius . . . and the stamina . . . of the Wright brothers . . . and their sister . . . what that family was able to give to the future. There were some words cast in stone . . . words that suggested that each family could . . . and should . . . give to the future . . . as the Wright family had. Which led to the words of the poem above.

Not every family can be as famous as the Wright family . . . and not every family can or will contribute to the genius of a nation . . . to the noted accomplishments of this world. Not all families will be recognized . . . immediately . . . for what they have bestowed to this world . . . or even to their own communities. We're not all going to be famous . . . we're not all going to have monuments erected to our names . . . or our family names . . . we're not all going to have books dedicated to our successes . . . those things are not going to happen to all of us . . . not even to many of us. Most will simply live their lives . . . within the love of their families . . . the family into which we were born . . . the family of friends . . . and co-workers . . . the school family

. . . the family of each house of worship. Families abound . . . and we will find ourselves within many . . . hopefully . . . all loving.

But . . . there is even a bigger family . . . the family of the children of the Most-High God . . . brothers and sisters of a large and distinguished family . . . whose Head is the very Creator of Heaven and earth . . . and all who and that inhabit His Creation.

Our family . . . and the families that form our family tree . . . the trunk . . . and limbs . . . and branches . . . our family . . . for which I am so blessed . . . is just one of the families that comprise His Creation . . . His Kingdom. We did not have all of the branches . . . of our family . . . represented this year . . . we missed those who could not attend . . . but those of us who did make it . . . were blessed to have been together . . . to have laughed together . . . to have shared together.

All families contribute to the beauty of this earth . . . all families are loved by our Creator . . . all sisters and brothers can make the world a more beautiful place . . . even if we have never met them . . . even if we have not witnessed their laughter . . . or their tears.

My Father . . . our Father . . . takes what each family does . . . what each family is . . . and threads that family . . . and their accomplishments . . . and their love . . . into a Tapestry of Beauty . . . and Love. Our Father Loves all families . . . Honors all families . . . and Forgives them their trespasses. We are all in this together . . . let us enjoy our family . . . and let us allow other families to enjoy theirs . . . whether they have a monument devoted to them . . . or not.

Though we/May control/The colors and shades/We repeat,/It is He/Who Designs/The Beauty of the Fabric/Complete.

TO BEGIN – August 2018

Father,
Open my eyes
To see
The world
As it is meant
To be.

Open my ears
To hear
The world
That could be
Oh, so near.

Open my heart
To feel
All the pain
Is gone;
All the love
Is real.

Let me not stumble;
Let me not fear;
Let me not forsake
Your children
So dear.

Then please,
Dear Father,
Let me step in;
And gain Your Trust
To do what I must
For Heaven on Earth
To begin.

I know it is here . . . real close . . . I can often feel it . . . occasionally see it . . . and if I'm quiet . . . I can hear it . . . Heaven on Earth. Sometimes . . . if I catch the last couple of minutes of the evening news . . . after all of the murders . . . natural disasters . . . political rhetoric . . . after all of the discord of this haunted world . . . I see a story of love and hope . . . of sisters and brothers being kind to each other . . . of community supporting each other . . . of good deeds . . . of sacrifice . . . and honor.

On those rare occasions . . . sitting out on the deck with a cup of coffee . . . when it's not raining . . . feeling a refreshing breeze . . . watching the sun peer around the house . . . listening to the songs of the birds . . .

as they get their morning start . . . it is then . . . not only then . . . but then . . . as I pray to my Lord . . . as I sit in His Grace and Bounty . . . as I witness the Beauty of His Truth . . . that I sense in my soul . . . the possibility of peace on earth . . . good will to all women and men . . . it is then that I can see the possibility of love overcoming hate . . . of discussion overcoming rhetoric . . . of sense overcoming fear . . . of a bond with nature that splits with destructive attitudes. My Lord lets me see . . . and hear . . . and feel . . . for just an instant . . . that peace on earth is a reality . . . somewhere . . . some time.

When I think of communities . . . with nothing . . . with little material possessions . . . with only each other with whom to trust . . . to share . . . to love . . . I think that we have probably missed the point of life. It is not about what we own . . . it is not the materialistic world that has our back. It is not nationalism . . . or organized religion . . . that brings us together. It is love for each other . . . it is sacrifice for each other . . . it is the caring and giving to each other . . . our sisters and brothers. It is in the acceptance that we are all different . . . born in different places . . . raised by different families . . . taught by different teachers . . . raised in different religions . . . all different . . . but all equal in His Sight. We have missed His Point . . . because we are focused on our greed . . . we are focused on our wants . . . not simply our needs.

Someday . . . we will learn to love Him with all of our heart, mind, soul and strength . . . we will learn to love our neighbors . . . our sisters and brothers . . . as ourselves . . . and we will get to the Promised Land . . . that Land of Light, Life and Love . . . that He Lets me glimpse every once in a while . . . and what a Beautiful Place It Is.

Then please,/Dear Father,/Let me step in;/And gain Your Trust/To do what I must/For Heaven on Earth/To begin.

YOUR MIRACLES – September 2018

Thank You,
Father,
For the Miracle
Of Your children.

Thank You

For that helpful hand.

Thank You
For that smile.

Thank You
For those prayers
That reach
Those distant miles.

Your children
Are a blessing
For which I reach
Each day.

Thank You,
Father,
For Your Miracles;
Who help me
Along the way.

There are so many good people in this world . . . but we seem to focus only on those we think are not-so-good.

This week has been a little more difficult for me than most. Had some outpatient surgery . . . which was probably successful . . . but which led to a rather long stint in the local university hospital emergency room. I'm really not complaining . . . I have no reason to complain . . . what is going on is due to my age . . . having gone past that milestone of three score and ten.

What I re-discovered this week . . . and I get angry with myself when I forget . . . is how wonderful His children are . . . my siblings in He Who Is my Lord. The doctors . . . the nurses . . . all of the hospital staff . . . so many . . . in so many different buildings . . . have been so good to me. So many times, I prayed for a miracle . . . and His children kept coming . . . with a smile . . . and a helping, sterilized hand . . . to get me through my fear . . . to get me some relief. I can't thank Him enough for those who serve their brothers and sisters. They are truly a blessing . . . they are truly a Miracle.

Your children/Are a blessing/For which I reach/Each day. Thank
You,/Father,/For Your Miracles;/Who help me/Along the way.

YOUR LOVE – October 2018

I pray,
Dear Lord,
That we may shout,
With one accord,
Your Love.

I pray,
Each day,
That we wake up
To say
He Loves us all;
The great,
The small;
He Loves us all.

I pray,
Dear Lord,
That we may hear
Your Word;
And shout it
Till we're hoarse;
And live it
Through our course.

I pray,
Each day,
That You
Will take away
All hate;
Before
It's all too late;
And we cement
Our fate.

I pray,
Dear Lord,
That we can look
Toward
A time
When all can heal;
A time
We can't conceal
Your Love.

I worship a Lord Who did not require social media to Teach and Preach His Message of Love and Forgiveness . . . Who did not even require a house of worship . . . especially an ornate one. I follow a Lord Who never asked for money . . . Who paid His taxes . . . and Lived by the laws of the land. I follow a Lord Who Preached and Taught on the hillside . . . or the water's edge . . . or on a small boat . . . or in a home. I follow a Lord Who Dined with the wealthy . . . and the poor . . . Who Took up for the lost and disenfranchised. I follow a Lord Who Served all . . . His followers . . . His students . . . the sick . . . the poor. I worship and follow a Lord Who spoke to everyone . . . and anyone . . . who wanted to . . . or needed to . . . listen . . . Who Spoke of His Father . . . our Father . . . Who Spoke of family and children . . . Who Spoke of love of all . . . who Spoke of forgiveness as many times as needed.

Things should be simpler . . . love the Lord God with all of our heart, soul, mind and strength . . . love our neighbors as ourselves . . . love our families (our closest neighbors) . . . forgive as we wish to be forgiven . . . live our lives in service to each other . . . that kind of simple.

I believe if we can concentrate on what my Lord Taught us as important . . . well . . . then the rest of all of the information . . . with which we are being bombarded . . . will be mostly noise . . . noise that we can filter to what is truly important . . . to us . . . to our families.

I pray,/Dear Lord,/That we can look/Toward/A time/When all can heal;/A time/We can't conceal/Your Love.

I CAN'T SEEM – January 2019

I make
My way
To Your Table,
Lord,
But there are still
A few things
On my mind.

I want
To love them
All
Like me;
But
I can't seem
To be that kind.

To wish them
Well
Is hard
To sell
This soul.

To wish them
Well
Should be
My life long
Goal.

So hard
For me
To see
All that
You See.

So hard
To know
What's right
Without

Your Sight.

Please let me see
As You
So I can see it
Through:
To walk along
And sing my song,
And let Your children
Sing theirs too.

A couple of things were going through my mind as I wrote the poem above this week. One was the older brother of the prodigal son . . . a lesson I have tried hard to learn over the years. The other was from my Lord's Sermon on the Mount . . . taken from The Gospel of Matthew . . . Chapter 5 . . . verses 22 through 24 . . . where my Lord said, "But I have added to that rule (if you murder, you must die), and tell you that if you are angry, even in your own home, you are in danger of judgement! If you call your friend an idiot, you are in danger of being brought before the court. And if you curse him, you are in danger of the fires of hell. So if you are standing before the alter in the Temple, offering a sacrifice to God, and suddenly remember that a friend has something against you, leave your sacrifice there beside the alter and go and apologize and be reconciled to him, and then come and offer your sacrifice to God." (from the Life Application Bible – The Living Bible).

Let me first discuss how the Prodigal Son's brother entered into my thinking. The Prodigal Son's brother . . . as I remember . . . was angry with his father for throwing a party for his brother . . . after his brother returned from spending all of his inheritance on wild living. But the Prodigal Son . . . when he returned . . . got down on his knees . . . seeking forgiveness from his father . . . and his father knew this prodigal son was sorry . . . truly sorry for his transgressions . . . and . . . the prodigal son asked for nothing from his father when he returned . . . it was his father's idea to throw a party. When the older brother confronted the father . . . and told his father that his father had never thrown him a party . . . his father simply said that he . . . the brother . . . could have had a party anytime he wanted . . . and that he . . . the brother . . . had had the privilege to live with his father the whole time

the prodigal son was gone. In other words . . . to me at least . . . why
would we . . . who love our relationship with our Father . . . and love to
be in His Presence . . . care if He should forgive . . . and take into His
Fold . . . someone . . . we believe . . . has spent their lives doing things
in which we don't believe. If I love my Father . . . and I love being
with my Father . . . then that should be enough.

Now . . . the second thing that entered my mind . . . murdering our
neighbor . . . our friends . . . with our words. My Lord said some very
hard things in his first recorded sermon in Matthew . . . the Sermon on
the Mount. Among His Teachings is the segment I've included in
paragraph 1. In this segment is the added emphasis on anger towards
our siblings . . . our Father's children . . . all of His children. Though
we may boast that we have never killed anyone . . . we need be careful
. . . for we may have destroyed them with our words . . . we may have
destroyed their reputation . . . we may have set them up for ridicule . . .
for bullying. We have no right to hurt another with our words . . . even
our thoughts are considered precious to our Father. So . . . if we have
hurt another . . . and we come to His Table . . . to be refreshed . . . to be
forgiven . . . then we need to go to anyone we have hurt . . . and ask for
their forgiveness . . . and we need to forgive those who trespass against
us . . . for He Said so . . . very clearly. We need to think before we
speak . . . we need to think before we act . . . sometimes we even need
to think before our thoughts go astray.

Others have the right to sing their own song . . . to live their own lives .
. . to believe as they have been taught . . . as they choose to believe.
Our Father Sees Differently than we see . . . He Loves all of His
children the same . . . even if we don't.

Please let me see/As You/So I can see it/Through:/To walk along/And
sing my song,/And let Your children/Sing theirs too.

WHY CAN'T WE? – March 2019

It is beginning
To warm.

The first robins
Have returned

To our yard.

The bulbs,
Lying beneath
The surface,
Are awakening;
Their leaves
Breaking the surface of
The softening earth.

New life
Is about
To thrill us
With its beauty.

Bright colors
Will remove
The grays
Of our discord.

A new season
Will appear;
So vibrant;
Oh, so dear.
...

Why can't we
Be as this;
Driving darkness out
With bliss?

Why can't we
Use our toil
To force bright leaves
Through hardened soil?

Why can't we
Bring new life:
With Love
Instead of strife?

Why can't we
Bring new mirth
To brighten other lives
On earth?

Why can't we
Bring forth
A new season
Full of human worth?

It's warming up in the east. Growth is beginning to peek through the once hardened ground. The cherry blossoms . . . along the Tidal Basin . . . should be in full bloom in another month. Not that it can't snow in March . . . or even early April . . . just that these first 70-degree days are really making me feel like Spring has sprung.

I walk around . . . outside . . . and see the crocus already with blooms . . . and see the jonquils forcing themselves to better light. The grass is beginning to turn . . . and I see some life on our pear trees . . . life which will bring us blooms . . . soon. Though Fall is probably still my favorite season, Spring is not far behind. I love how new life begins after a winter of freezing rain and cold.

I watch the news . . . blizzards in the Rockies . . . high winds and tornadoes in the South. I see the people . . . in those stories . . . shaking their heads . . . in tears . . . declaring they will rebuild again. That's the way it is with most of us. When nature deals us a blow . . . we rebuild . . . whether it be floods . . . or tornadoes . . . or fire . . . we stand our ground. Like the flowers reclaiming their rightful place . . . in the Spring . . . humanity tends to take their seasons in stride . . . with the stamina to rebuild.

But that is the human response to Nature. Why would humans want to destroy each other . . . when Nature does a good enough job by itself? If I continue to watch the news . . . which I probably shouldn't . . . then I see mass shootings . . . in my country of origin . . . and in other countries. Since I get the Washington, D.C. news here . . . I see shootings every day in the Capital . . . humans taking other human lives. I also see hatred abounding . . . for . . . obviously . . . to me at least . . . human worth is not equal in the eyes of many . . . some feeling they are worth so much more than others . . . why they hate . . . why they kill. I don't get it . . . I never will.

If my Father . . . in Heaven . . . is everyone else's Father in Heaven . . . if those I see . . . anywhere . . . and everywhere . . . are my sister . . . or my brother . . . why would I want harm to come to them? Though sisters and brothers do not always get along . . . harm to one or the other should never be an option. Though misunderstandings may occur . . . hatred should never be an option either. We cannot always agree . . . but . . . I believe . . . we can always . . . at least . . . tolerate . . . maybe even listen to each other.

Every Spring . . . I see new life . . . life that comes through the hardships of winter. We have hardships enough due to the elements of Nature. Why can't we help each other through those hardships? Why can't we respect each other . . . whether we agree with each other . . . or not? All of the blooms . . . that last through the bitter Winter . . . that come into bloom with Spring . . . have their individual worth. Why can't we?

SUCH A WASTE – September 2019

Such a waste:
To love our possessions
And not our neighbors;
To love the things
That hands have made;
But not the hands
Of those who made them.

I have wrestled with this often. We love our stuff . . . but not necessarily those who made our stuff. We so often love things more than our brothers and sisters . . . those we see . . . and those we don't see.

It makes no sense to me . . . how we could love our car . . . yet hurt someone with it . . . how we could love an article of clothing . . . or maybe a piece of jewelry . . . yet have no love for someone . . . or maybe have animosity . . . toward someone . . . of another belief . . . or color . . . or nationality . . . who made . . . or fashioned . . . that very article of clothing . . . or piece of jewelry . . . that we love so much. Maybe we dislike another because we haven't met them yet . . . maybe we have no knowledge . . . nor do we care to have any knowledge . . . of someone . . . not like us . . . who makes those things we love the most. Maybe we don't even want to think about the people who provide us with those things which we love. Maybe we don't want to think about people at all.

Though I still love my Lord with all of my heart, mind, soul and strength . . . and I try hard to love my neighbor as I love myself . . . yet I fear . . . so very much . . . that the love of things is making gains on the love of His children.

Such a waste:/To love our possessions/And not our neighbors;/To love the things/That hands have made;/But not the hands/Of those who made them.

RESPECT WE GIVE - September 2019

Respect we give
If in peace
To live.

We need not
Agree
With one another;
Though
We should listen.

We were not raised
The same;
We come
From different places.

Though
We are closer
To each other
Than we think.

Though
We may not look
The same,
We are made
In His Image;
Not in ours.

We are siblings,
With One Parent.

He Looks Down
From Above
With Love.

He Respects
Not one
Over another.

We need look
With no despise
Into the eyes
Of our siblings.

Respect we give
If in peace
To live.

Nan and I have had many discussions concerning respect in our past. In the 52 years we've been married, there were times when we didn't particularly like each other . . . but we still respected each other. One would hope that love was always the cornerstone of our relationship . . . however . . . I think respect may have been a large part of our foundation. Being in love is one thing . . . respecting the person we love is another thing altogether.

I believe part of the concept in "love your neighbor as yourself" is the idea . . . or ideal . . . of respect. If love is too hard a term to place on our neighbor . . . a neighbor we don't even know . . . then maybe we could say respect our neighbor . . . until we know them better . . . and love becomes more meaningful.

Unless we are siblings of the same earthly parents, we do not know the household development of our universe sisters and brothers. We do not know how they were raised . . . in what environment . . . under what hardships. We do not know their trauma . . . we do not know their heartaches. We simply do not know what has happened in their lives . . . how they have been treated . . . how they see the world . . . from their frame of reference. But . . . we can respect them for making it as far as they have . . . we can respect them for their contributions to their own families . . . we can respect them for surviving in an unfair world.

We need not despise those we do not know . . . how much better to show them some respect . . . until love becomes a way of life.

Now . . . I have stated often in the past . . . there are two quotes from my Lord that changed the way I view our Father. The first quote . . . "The rain falls on the just and unjust" . . . gives me a hint of His Impartiality. Whether we see rain as good or bad . . . the message is still clear . . . some bad will fall on the just . . . and some good will fall on the unjust . . . it doesn't matter what we think . . . we have no say in the matter. The second quote . . . "The Father in no Respecter of persons" . . . may prove my premise incorrect in relation to simply respecting each other. But . . . I don't think my Lord meant for us not to respect others . . . I believe He Meant our Father does not look more favorably on one than another . . . His Love is True . . . He Loves all the same . . . no matter what we think . . . no matter what we've been taught. We may think more highly of ourselves . . . or our family . . . or our race . . . or our creed . . . or our nationality . . . but He Does Not. He does not respect one over another . . . and He is impartial to those we believe to be good or bad.

We have been made in His Image . . . but we want so much for Him to be made in ours.

Respect we give/If in peace/To live.

MY EYES MIST – October 2019

My eyes mist

As I think of this:
That we have modified
The story
Of His Love and Glory;
That we have dissolved
Love
Into a mixture of
Jealousy and hate;
And we can't wait
To point the finger
At those
Who are simply different
Than we;
That we have decided
That the rain falls
Only
On the unjust;
And we have decided
Who the unjust are;
And what the rain should be
For those simply different
Than we.

I can only sigh
When I think of what
We have done
With His Song;
When I think how wrong
We have become
With a Truth
Once so Pure and Sure.

I graduated from high school in the mid 1960's . . . went to college through the late 1960's . . . so I know how bad society can act to times of change. The 1960's were brutal . . . not unlike the now . . . civil unrest was rampant . . . we were fighting a war few understood . . . there weren't as many mass shootings as there were mass beatings . . . and there were more than enough assassinations to some beloved movers of change.

124

More people went to church back in the 1960's . . . so I'm not sure church going is a factor in a brutal society . . . except maybe for the hope given to the down trodden.

Changing subjects . . . in history . . . going all the way back to Abraham . . . the One-God concept was taught to a select few . . . with the promise of good things to come for those who would follow the One True God. Moses worked to continue and deepen the understanding of Who the One-God Was . . . and Is . . . the Great I Am. The later prophets made additional headway in the development of the One True God . . . by replacing the need for sacrifice with love . . . love for each other.

Finally . . . my Lord Came down to further paint the picture of the One True God . . . also known as Jehovah . . . and Allah . . . and The Great Spirit . . . and Father in Heaven . . . among other Names by peoples around the world . . . as a Loving Father . . . a Father Who Rejoices as His children turn to Him.

Throughout the journey to understand, it was always about Love . . . our love for Him . . . His Love for us . . . even throughout the testing of rules . . . countless rules . . . to keep the people in check . . . while the maturation of the One True God concept took place. No matter the religion . . . it has always been about Love.

So . . . how could we take a Truth so Pure . . . and turn that Truth into jealousy and hate? Why can't we all see that our Father . . . called by many names . . . Who Made us in His Image . . . is the Source of Love . . . is the Giver of Love . . . is the I Am of Love?

We make Him into our own image . . . and fill Him with Jealousy . . . and Hate . . . and Anger. It is our jealousy . . . and hate . . . and anger . . . that fills this earth . . . not His. He Loves us . . . He Always Has . . . and I'm not sure why . . .

I can only sigh/When I think of what/We have done/With His Song;/When I think how wrong/We have become/With a Truth/Once so Pure and Sure.

SO MANY – October 2019

So many words
Have been written
To praise Him
And explain Him;
So many poems
And psalms,
Manuscripts and Books,
Short verse and long verse,
Metaphors and analogies
Placed together
In His Honor.

So many musical notes
Have been written
To sing His Praise;
To lift our spirits;
So many songs and hymns,
Classics and rock,
Short and long
For solo or throng
To bring joy to our hearts
And tears to our eyes
As we sing our praises
To Him.

So many strokes
Of a brush
Have been placed
On canvas or wall
Or fresco
To depict His Love
And His Sacrifice
For our souls;
They too tug at our hearts
As we stand in awe
Before them;
As we experience the creativity
Of the artist

In the pictures
That portray His Beauty.

So many acres of land
Have been bought,
And buildings of great stature
Have been built
In His Name;
Landscaped and erected
To bring the masses
Into His Presence
So that they can worship Him.

So many prayers
Line the corridors of Heaven;
Requesting help,
Seeking favor,
Asking forgiveness
For ourselves
And for others,

We want to show Him
How much we love Him;
Yet we neglect His children
For whom
He Has Built Great Mansions.

Not sure how much more I can say about the poem above. It's meaning to me is great . . . I have pondered the issue for decades . . . it is clear to me our folly

Countless hours have been spent creating for the Most-High God. Billions and Trillions . . . of whatever currency has been spent on land . . . and buildings . . . and gold . . . and silver . . . and artwork . . . to decorate those buildings . . . as a tribute to the Most-High God.

Yet . . . we neglect the very children He Loves. We take advantage of the very children He Loves. We ridicule the very children He Loves. We treat the very children He Loves as dirt. How much better it would be to show we love Him by loving and respecting all of His children.

And . . . all the while we treat His children as inferior beings . . . He Builds the very Mansions . . . with Heavenly Rooms . . . for them to rest their weary heads.

We have it all wrong . . . we always have . . . we simply can't see Him for Who He Is . . . The I Am . . . the Creator of Heaven and earth . . . Who Is no respecter of persons . . . and Who Loves all of His children equally.

We want to show Him/How much we love Him;/Yet we neglect His children/For whom He has built great mansions.

LOVING YOU – February 2020

Loving You
Is easy.

Loving Your children
Is not.

Loving You
Takes no strength
At all.

Loving them
Takes all
I got.

The poem above is one of those that really doesn't require much of a message . . . it kind of says it all for me.

I have been saying . . . and teaching . . . for decades . . . that of the two greatest commandments . . . loving the Lord your God with all of your heart, mind, soul and strength and loving your neighbor as yourself . . . the former is relatively easy . . . especially for believers . . . but the latter . . . I don't believe . . . will ever be easy . . . at least in my lifetime.

This becomes ever so apparent during an election year . . . when most . . . who are running . . . spend more time tearing down their opponents .

. . and less time discussing their own agenda. It doesn't help . . . me at least . . . to have spent most of my adult life . . . either watching Philadelphia or Washington D.C. news . . . where hours and hours are spent reporting horrible things. Nan and I are doing our best to watch the shows we have recorded during the afternoon and evening news.

God's children are good . . . we all have it in us to love one another. What I will never get is if we truly love the Lord God with all of our hearts, minds, soul and strength . . . then why can't we love all of His children . . . at least respect them . . . no matter their skin color . . . their religion . . . their nationality? If we truly love . . . or loved our parents . . . did we not love all of their children . . . our natural siblings? We may not have always liked them . . . but do we not always love them . . . wish them no harm?

The two greatest commandments are recorded for a reason. If we follow those two . . . all of the other commandments fall into place.

TO SEE HIM SMILE – February 2020

I was born here;
But,
This is not my Home.

My journey
Has taken me here;
But,
This is not
My destination.

I am to learn here
To love
My sisters and brothers.

I am to teach here
The Love
Of our Heavenly Father.

I am to be
A good and faithful servant

Before
I can ever go Home.

The journey
Is not an easy one;
But,
To see Him Smile
Will make it worthwhile.

I believe that I am in school . . . and that the lessons are hard. I believe that we all are.

I am not sure how it all works . . . maybe I will learn back Home . . . but I was born here . . . as an adopted child of my birth parents. An Infinitely Small Piece of my Father . . . in Heaven . . . was placed into my small being . . . to be connected to Him . . . and be a magnet . . . ever drawn to Him. My birth place . . . where I made my start . . . however . . . wherever I was born . . . whatever color I was . . . whatever nationality I became . . . was right here . . . on earth. I cannot change my color . . . my nationality . . . where I was born . . . my birth parents . . . my upbringing . . . my birth siblings. I can change nothing about how I was raised . . . my religious training . . . the local schools I attended.

All I can do . . . is learn from my beginnings. All I can do is to put it all in perspective . . . my journey to this point . . . the journey of my three score and thirteen years.

My principal job . . . here . . . is to learn how to be a good child . . . and a good sibling. My principal responsibilities . . . here . . . are to Him . . . and His children. My journey weaves through that job . . . and those responsibilities. I go to school . . . with His children . . . I go to work . . . with His children . . . my play . . . is with His children . . . indeed . . . I am surrounded by His children . . . who were brought up by different earth parents . . . who are of different colors . . . different religions . . . different nationalities . . . it doesn't matter . . . they are His children . . . and my journey includes them . . . passes through them.

When I am through this journey . . . which I am mostly through . . . if I have treated His children as I have wished to be treated . . . if I have treated them as loving siblings . . . then I can go Home . . . and meet my Father . . . and hear Him Say, "Well done . . . good and faithful servant . . . welcome Home."

The journey/Is not an easy one;/But,/To see Him Smile/Will make it worthwhile.